THE KNITTER'S BIBLE

Stitch Library

THE KNITTER'S BIBLE

Stitch Library

CLAIRE CROMPTON

D&C

David and Charles

www.rucraft.co.uk

A DAVID & CHARLES BOOK
Copyright © David & Charles Limited 2010

David & Charles is an F+W Media Inc. company
4700 East Galbraith Road, Cincinnati, OH 45236

First published in the UK and US in 2010

Text and designs copyright © Claire Crompton 2010

A catalogue record for this book is available from the
British Library.

ISBN-13: 978-0-7153-3776-9 paperback
ISBN-10: 0-7153-3776-9 paperback

Printed in China by RR Donnelley
for David & Charles
Brunel House, Newton Abbot, Devon

Publisher Alison Myer
Acquisitions Editor Jennifer Fox-Proverbs
Editor James Brooks
Project Editor Lorraine Slipper
Designer Victoria Marks
Photographer Karl Adamson and Lorna Yabsley
Production Controller Kelly Smith
Pre Press Natasha Jorden

David & Charles publish high quality books on a wide
range of subjects. For more great book ideas visit:
www.rucraft.co.uk

CONTENTS

INTRODUCTION

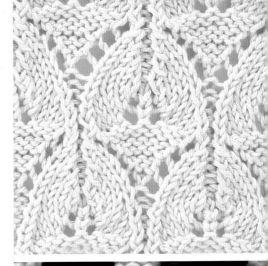

This book offers you a fully comprehensive collection of knitting stitches, ranging from the very simple to the most complex, the traditional to the new and innovative. Use it as a guide to making your own unique knitted pieces, whether you are creating beautiful garments, useful accessories or stylish adornments for your home.

The Stitch Library (see pages 10–95) begins with simple but effective knit and purl stitches that add subtle texture to a plain garment. These include traditional Gansey (or Guernsey) patterns, with advice on how to use them to design your own classic sweaters. Using texture stitches, cable panels and fabrics, and embossed fabrics, you can make up more tactile and three-dimensional pieces. Elegant colour patterns can be created using slip stitches, dip stitches and stripes. For openwork pieces, you will find lace stitches and panels, together with eyelets and drop stitch patterns. Use the range of edgings and borders to give an individual touch to your next knitted garment or to personalize your ready-made clothing by adding a knitted trim.

The Projects section (see pages 96–127) will give you a range of ideas about how to use the stitches, with suggestions for designing your own versions. Use these projects to inspire you; the Cable Throw (page 101) could just as easily be worked in panels of lace or texture stitches. The Making Waves scarf (page 119) shows how a simple wave stitch can be worked in two yarns for a stunning effect.

It's All in the Detail (see pages 128–141) takes you through the basics of knit and purl stitch, how to cast on and bind off, increasing and decreasing stitches and more, so it is worth reading this before you pick up your needles to begin. Each stitch has full instructions and a clear stitch chart where appropriate, making it easier to see how to work each row. Use the charts together with the keys; you will find advice on how to work from the charts on page 140.

Experiment with the stitches, try something new, mix them up and create your own style.

STITCH LIBRARY

KNIT AND PURL STITCHES

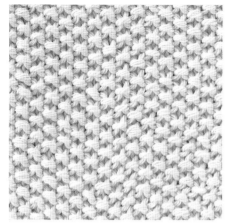

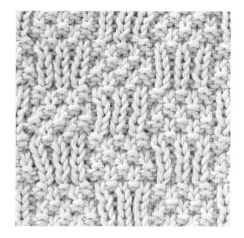

Moss Stitch (reversible)

On an odd number of stitches.
Row 1 K1, * p1, k1; rep from * to end.
Repeat this row.

On an even number of stitches.
Row 1 * K1, p1; rep from * to end.
Row 2 * P1, k1; rep from * to end.
Repeat these 2 rows.

Double Moss Stitch (reversible)

On an odd number of stitches.
Row 1 K1, * p1, k1; rep from * to end.
Row 2 P1, * k1, p1; rep from * to end.
Row 3 As row 2.
Row 4 As row 1.
Repeat these 4 rows.

On an even number of stitches.
Row 1 * K1, p1; rep from * to end.
Row 2 As row 1.
Row 3 * P1, k1; rep from * to end.
Row 4 As row 3.
Repeat these 4 rows.

Double Moss Stitch and Rib Check (reversible)

Multiple of 12 sts plus 7.
Row 1 * (P1, k1) 3 times, p2, (k1, p1) twice; rep from * to last 7 sts, (p1, k1) 3 times, p1.
Row 2 K1, (p1, k1) 3 times, * (k1, p1) twice, k2, (p1, k1) 3 times; rep from * to end.
Row 3 P1, * k1, p1; rep from * to end.
Row 4 K1, * p1, k1; rep from * to end.
Row 5 As row 1.
Row 6 As row 2.
Row 7 * P2, k1, p1, k1, p2, (k1, p1) twice, k1; rep from * to last 7 sts, p2, k1, p1, k1, p2.
Row 8 K2, p1, k1, p1, k2, * (p1, k1) twice, p1, k2, p1, k1, p1, k2; rep from * to end.
Row 9 As row 3.
Row 10 As row 4.
Row 11 As row 7.
Row 12 As row 8.
Repeat these 12 rows.

Stitch library charts

Stitch charts have been included for most of the stitches in the library, apart from those where increasing and decreasing a number of stitches makes a chart difficult to follow.

You can use the stitch charts to design your own garments, work out increases and decreases in pattern, design your own cable panels or put together gansey sweater designs.

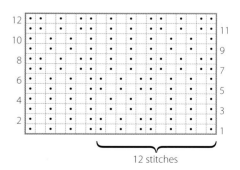

12 stitches

KEY

• p on RS rows, k on WS rows

☐ k on RS rows, p on WS rows

KNIT AND PURL STITCHES

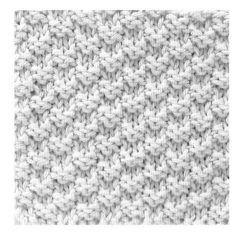

Two Stitch Check
(reversible)

Multiple of 4 sts plus 2.
Row 1 K2, * p2, k2; rep from * to end.
Row 2 P2, * k2, p2; rep from * to end.
Row 3 As row 2.
Row 4 As row 1.
Repeat these 4 rows.

Four Stitch Check
(reversible)

Multiple of 8 sts.
Rows 1, 2, 3 and 4 * K4, p4; rep from * to end.
Rows 5, 6, 7 and 8 * P4, k4; rep from * to end.
Repeat these 8 rows.

Basketweave

Multiple of 8 sts plus 5.
Row 1 (RS) Knit.
Row 2 * K5, p3; rep from * to last 5 sts, k5.
Row 3 P5, * k3, p5; rep from * to end.
Row 4 As row 2.
Row 5 Knit.
Row 6 K1, p3, k1, * k4, p3, k1; rep from * to end.
Row 7 * P1, k3, p4; rep from * to last 5 sts, p1, k3, p1.
Row 8 As row 6.
Repeat these 8 rows.

4 stitches

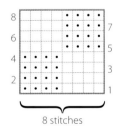

8 stitches

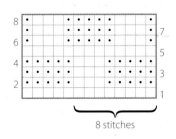

8 stitches

KEY

· p on RS rows, k on WS rows
☐ k on RS rows, p on WS rows

KNIT AND PURL STITCHES

Double Basketweave

Multiple of 18 sts plus 10.
Row 1 (RS) Knit.
Row 2 P10, * p1, k2, p2, k2, p11; rep from * to end.
Row 3 * K1, p8, (k2, p2) twice, k1; rep from * to last 10 sts, k1, p8, k1.
Row 4 P1, k8, p1, * p1, (k2, p2) twice, k8, p1; rep from * to end.
Row 5 * K11, p2, k2, p2, k1; rep from * to last 10 sts, k10.
Row 6 As row 2.
Row 7 As row 3.
Row 8 As row 4.
Row 9 As row 5.
Row 10 Purl.
Row 11 * (K2, p2) twice, k10; rep from * to last 10 sts, k2, (p2, k2) twice.
Row 12 P2, (k2, p2) twice, * k8, p2, (k2, p2) twice; rep from * to end.
Row 13 * K2, (p2, k2) twice, p8; rep from * to last 10 sts, k2, (p2, k2) twice.
Row 14 P2, (k2, p2) twice, * p10, (k2, p2) twice; rep from * to end.
Row 15 As row 11.
Row 16 As row 12.
Row 17 As row 13.
Row 18 As row 14.
Repeat these 18 rows.

Pennant

Multiple of 7 sts plus 1.
Row 1 (RS) K1, * p1, k6; rep from * to end.
Row 2 * P5, k2; rep from * to last st, p1.
Row 3 K1, * p3, k4; rep from * to end.
Row 4 P3, k4; rep from * to last st, p1.
Row 5 K1, * p5, k2; rep from * to end.
Row 6 P1, * k6, p1; rep from * to end.
Repeat these 6 rows.

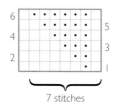

7 stitches

Pyramid

Multiple of 6 sts plus 1.
Row 1 (RS) * K1, p5; rep from * to last st, k1.
Row 2 P1, * k5, p1; rep from * to end.
Row 3 * K2, p3, k1; rep from * to last st, k1.
Row 4 P1, * p1, k3, p2; rep from * to end.
Row 5 * K3, p1, k2; rep from * to last st, k1.
Row 6 P1, * p2, k1, p3; rep from * to end.
Row 7 * P3, k1, p2; rep from * to last st, p1.
Row 8 K1, * k2, p1, k3; rep from * to end.
Row 9 * P2, k3, p1; rep from * to last st, p1.
Row 10 K1, * k1, p3, k2; rep from * to end.
Row 11 * P1, k5; rep from * to last st, p1.
Row 12 K1, * p5, k1; rep from * to end.
Repeat these 12 rows.

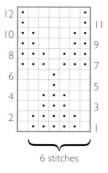

6 stitches

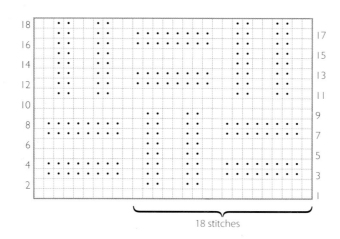

18 stitches

KEY

· p on RS rows, k on WS rows
☐ k on RS rows, p on WS rows

KNIT AND PURL STITCHES

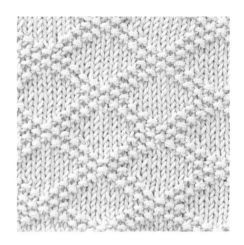

Moss Stitch Diamonds

Multiple of 6 sts plus 1.
Row 1 (RS) * K3, p1, k2; rep from * to last st, k1.
Row 2 P1, * (p1, k1) twice, p2; rep from * to end.
Rows 3, 4 and 5 * K1, p1; rep from * to last st, k1.
Row 6 As row 2.
Repeat these 6 rows.

Moss Stitch Rib

Multiple of 10 sts plus 1.
Row 1 (RS) * K4, p1, k1, p1, k3; rep from * to last st, k1.
Row 2 P1, * p2, (k1, p3) twice; rep from * to end.
Row 3 * K2, (p1, k1) 4 times; rep from * to last st, k1.
Row 4 P1, * k1, p1, k1, p3, (k1, p1) twice; rep from * to end.
Row 5 As row 3.
Row 6 As row 2.
Repeat these 6 rows.

King Charles Brocade

Multiple of 12 sts plus 1.
Row 1 (RS) *K1, p1, k9, p1; rep from * to last st, k1.
Row 2 K1, * p1, k1, p7, k1, p1, k1; rep from * to end.
Row 3 * (K1, p1) twice, k5, p1, k1, p1; rep from * to last st, k1.
Row 4 P1, * (p1, k1) twice, p3, k1, p1, k1, p2; rep from * to end.
Row 5 * K3, p1, (k1, p1) 3 times, k2; rep from * to last st, k1.
Row 6 P1, * p3, k1, (p1, k1) twice, p4; rep from * to end.
Row 7 * K5, p1, k1, p1, k4; rep from * to last st, k1.
Row 8 As row 6.
Row 9 As row 5.
Row 10 As row 4.
Row 11 As row 3.
Row 12 As row 2.
Repeat these 12 rows.

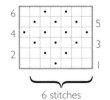

6 stitches

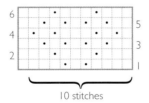

10 stitches

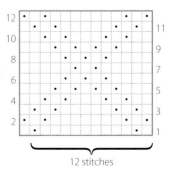

12 stitches

KEY

· p on RS rows, k on WS rows
☐ k on RS rows, p on WS rows

KNIT AND PURL STITCHES

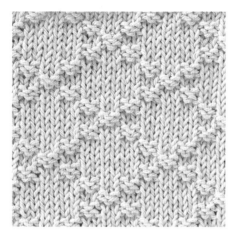

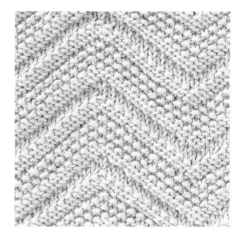

Stepped Diamonds

Multiple of 12 sts plus 2.

Row 1 (RS) * P2, k10; rep from * to last 2 sts, p2.

Row 2 K2, * p10, k2; rep from * to end.

Row 3 * K2, p2, k6, p2; rep from * to last 2 sts, k2.

Row 4 P2, * k2, p6, k2, p2; rep from * to end.

Row 5 * K4, p2, k2, p2, k2; rep from * to last 2 sts, k2.

Row 6 P2, * (p2, k2) twice, p4; rep from * to end.

Row 7 * K6, p2, k4; rep from * to last 2 sts, k2.

Row 8 P2, * p4, k2, p6; rep from * to end.

Row 9 As row 5.

Row 10 As row 6.

Row 11 As row 3.

Row 12 As row 4.

Repeat these 12 rows.

Mock Cable (reversible)

Multiple of 10 sts.

Row 1 * P4, k1, p1, k4; rep from * to end.

Row 2 *P3, k2, p2, k3; rep from * to end.

Row 3 * P2, k2, p1, k1, p2, k2; rep from * to end.

Row 4 * P1, (k2, p2) twice, k1; rep from * to end.

Row 5 * K2, p3, k3, p2; rep from * to end.

Row 6 * K1, p4, k4, p1; rep from * to end.

Repeat these 6 rows.

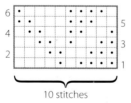

10 stitches

Moss Stitch Chevron

Multiple of 22 sts plus 1.

Row 1 (RS) * K1, p3, k1, (p1, k1) twice, p5, k1, (p1, k1) twice, p3; rep from * to last st, k1.

Row 2 P1, * p1, k3, p1, (k1, p1) twice, k3, p1, (k1, p1) twice, k3, p2; rep from * to end.

Row 3 K3, p3, k1, (p1, k1) 5 times, p3, k2; rep from * to last st, k1.

Row 4 K1, * p3, k3, p1, (k1, p1) 4 times, k3, p3, k1; rep from * to end.

Row 5 * P2, k3, p3, k1, (p1, k1) 3 times, p3, k3, p1; rep from * to last st, p1.

Row 6 K1, * k2, p3, k3, p1, (k1, p1) twice, k3, p3, k3; rep from * to end.

Row 7 * K1, p3, k3, p3, k1, p1, k1, p3, k3, p3; rep from * to last st, k1.

Row 8 K1, * p1, k3, p3, k3, p1, k3, p3, k3, p1, k1; rep from * to end.

Row 9 * K1, p1, k1, p3, k3, p5, k3, p3, k1, p1; rep from * to last st, k1.

Row 10 K1, * p1, k1, p1, (k3, p3) twice, k3, (p1, k1) twice; rep from * to end.

Row 11 * K1, (p1, k1) twice, p3, k3, p1, k3, p3, (k1, p1) twice; rep from * to last st, k1.

Row 12 K1, * p1, (k1, p1) twice, k3, p5, k3, (p1, k1) 3 times; rep from * to end.

Row 13 * P2, k1, (p1, k1) twice, p3, k3, p3, (k1, p1) 3 times; rep from * to last st, p1.

Row 14 K1, * k2, p1, (k1, p1) twice, k3, p1, k3, p1, (k1, p1) twice, k3; rep from * to end.

Repeat these 14 rows.

KEY

- p on RS rows, k on WS rows
- k on RS rows, p on WS rows

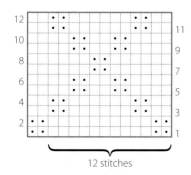

12 stitches

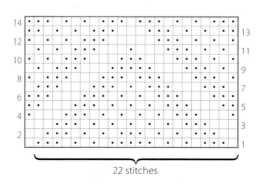

22 stitches

KNIT AND PURL STITCHES

Small Gingham (reversible)

Multiple of 10 sts plus 5.
Row 1 * P5, k1, (p1, k1) twice; rep from * to last 5 sts, p5.
Row 2 K5, * (k1, p1) twice, k6; rep from * to end.
Rows 3 to 6 Repeat rows 1 and 2 twice more.
Row 7 * (K1, p1) twice, k6; rep from * to last 5 sts, (k1, p1) twice, k1.
Row 8 K1, (p1, k1) twice, * p5, k1, (p1, k1) twice; rep from * to end.
Rows 9 to 12 Repeat rows 7 and 8 twice more.
Repeat these 12 rows.

Gingham Check

Multiple of 14 sts plus 9.
Row 1 (RS) * (K1, p1) 4 times, k1, p5; rep from * to last 9 sts, (k1, p1) 4 times, k1.
Row 2 (K1, p1) 4 times, k1, * k6, (p1, k1) 4 times; rep from * to end.
Rows 3 to 5 Repeat rows 1 and 2 once more then row 1 again.
Row 6 P9, * (p1, k1) twice, p10; rep from * to end.
Row 7 * K9, (p1, k1) twice, p1; rep from * to last 9 sts, k9.
Rows 8 to 15 Repeat rows 6 and 7 four times more.
Row 16 As row 6.
Repeat these 16 rows.

Heart Squares

Multiple of 14 sts plus 1.
Row 1 (RS) * P1, k1; rep from * to last st, p1.
Row 2 Purl.
Row 3 * P1, k6; rep from * to last st, p1.
Row 4 P1, * p5, k3, p6; rep from * to end.
Row 5 * P1, k4, p2, k1, p2, k4; rep from * to last st, p1.
Row 6 P1, * (p3, k2) twice, p4; rep from * to end.
Row 7 * P1, k2, p2, k5, p2, k2; rep from * to last st, p1.
Row 8 P1, * p1, k2, p3, k1, p3, k2, p2; rep from * to end.
Row 9 * P1, k1, p2, k2, p3, k2, p2, k1; rep from * to last st, p1.
Row 10 P1, * p2, k4, p1, k4, p3; rep from * to end.
Row 11 * P1, (k3, p2) twice, k3; rep from * to last st, p1.
Row 12 Purl.
Repeat these 12 rows.

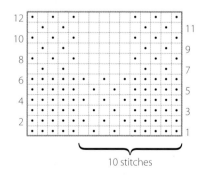

10 stitches

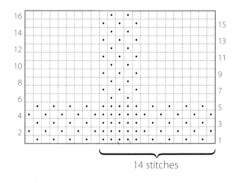

14 stitches

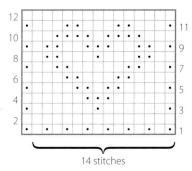

14 stitches

KEY

- ⊡ p on RS rows, k on WS rows
- ☐ k on RS rows, p on WS rows

KNIT AND PURL STITCHES

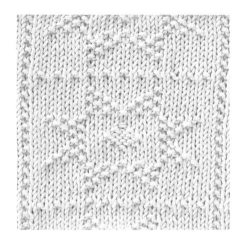

Star in a Square

Multiple of 24 sts plus 1.

Row 1 (RS) * P1, k1; rep from * to last st, p1.

Row 2 Purl.

Row 3 * P1, k23; rep from * to last st, p1.

Row 4 P1, * (p7, k1) twice, p8; rep from * to end.

Row 5 * P1, k8, p1, k5, p1, k8; rep from * to last st, p1.

Row 6 P1, * p7, k1, p1, k1, p3, k1, p1, k1, p8; rep from * to end.

Row 7 * P1, k8, p1, (k1, p1) 3 times, k8; rep from * to last st, p1.

Row 8 P1, * p7, k1, (p1, k1) 4 times, p8; rep from * to end.

Row 9 * P1, k2, p1, (k1, p1) twice, k9, p1, (k1, p1) twice, k2; rep from * to last st, p1.

Row 10 P1, * p3, k1, p1, k1, p11, k1, p1, k1, p4; rep from * to end.

Row 11 * P1, k4, p1, k1, (p1, k4) twice, p1, k1, p1, k4; rep from * to last st, p1.

Row 12 P1, * p5, k1, p4, k3, p4, k1, p6; rep from * to end.

Row 13 * P1, k6, p1, k2, p5, k2, p1, k6; rep from * to last st, p1.

Row 14 As row 12.

Row 15 As row 11.

Rows 16 to 23 Work from row 10 back to row 3.

Row 24 Purl.

Repeat these 24 rows.

Tumbling Blocks

Multiple of 10 sts.

Row 1 * K1, p1; rep from * to end.

Row 2 * P1, k1, p1, k2, p2, k1, p1, k1; rep from * to end.

Row 3 * K1, p1, k3, p3, k1, p1; rep from * to end.

Row 4 * P1, k4, p4, k1; rep from * to end.

Row 5 * K5, p5; rep from * to end.

Rows 6 to 8 Repeat row 5, 3 times more.

Row 9 * K4, p1, k1, p4; rep from * to end.

Row 10 * K3, (p1, k1) twice, p3; rep from * to end.

Row 11 * K2, (p1, k1) 3 times, p2; rep from * to end.

Row 12 * K1, p1; rep from * to end.

Row 13 * P1, k1; rep from * to end.

Row 14 * P2, (k1, p1) 3 times, k2; rep from * to end.

Row 15 * P3, (k1, p1) twice, k3; rep from * to end.

Row 16 * P4, k1, p1, k4; rep from * to end.

Row 17 * P5, k5; rep from * to end.

Rows 18 to 20 Repeat row 17, 3 times more.

Row 21 * K1, p4, k4, p1; rep from * to end.

Row 22 * P1, k1, p3, k3, p1, k1; rep from * to end.

Row 23 * K1, p1, k1, p2, k2, p1, k1, p1; rep from * to end.

Row 24 * P1, k1; rep from * to end.

Repeat these 24 rows.

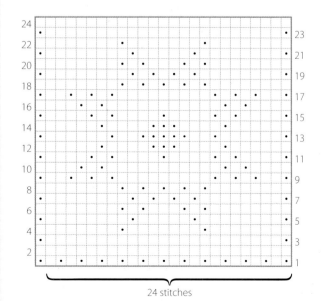

24 stitches

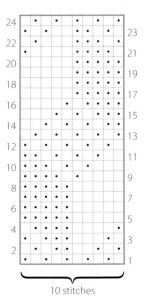

10 stitches

KNIT AND PURL STITCHES

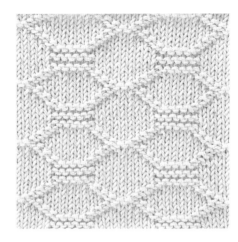

Star in a Diamond

Multiple of 32 sts plus 1.

Row 1 (RS) * P1, (k1, p1) 3 times, k9, p1, k9, (p1, k1) 3 times; rep from * to last st, p1.

Row 2 P1, * k1, (p1, k1) 3 times, p7, k1, p1, k1, p7, (k1, p1) 4 times; rep from * to end.

Row 3 * P1, (k1, p1) 4 times, k5, p1, k3, p1, k5, (p1, k1) 4 times; rep from * to last st, p1.

Row 4 P1, * k1, (p1, k1) 4 times, p3, k1, p5, k1, p3, (k1, p1) 5 times; rep from * to end.

Row 5 * P1, (k1, p1) 6 times, k7, (p1, k1) 6 times; rep from * to last st, p1.

Row 6 P1, * k1, p1, k1, p7, k1, p9, k1, p7, (k1, p1) twice; rep from * to end.

Row 7 * P1, (k1, p1) twice, k5, p1, k1, p1, k7, p1, k1, p1, k5, (p1, k1) twice; rep from * to last st, p1.

Row 8 P1, * k1, p1, k1, p5, k1, p3, k1, p5, k1, p3, k1, p5, (k1, p1) twice; rep from * to end.

Row 9 * K2, p1, k1, p1, (k3, p1) twice, k1, p1, k3, p1, k1, (p1, k3) twice, (p1, k1) twice; rep from * to last st, k1.

Row 10 P1, * p2, k1, p3, k1, p5, (k1, p1) 3 times, k1, p5, (k1, p3) twice; rep from * to end.

Row 11 * K4, p1, k1, p1, k5, p1, (k1, p1) 4 times, k5, p1, k1, p1, k3; rep from * to last st, k1.

Row 12 P1, * p4, k1, p7, k1, (p1, k1) 3 times, p7, k1, p5; rep from * to end.

Row 13 * K4, p1, (k1, p1) 12 times, k3; rep from * to last st, k1.

Row 14 P1, * p2, k1, p3, k1, (p1, k1) 9 times, p3, k1, p3; rep from * to end.

Row 15 * K2, p1, k5, p1, (k1, p1) 8 times, k5, p1, k1; rep from * to last st, k1.

Row 16 P1, * k1, p7, k1, (p1, k1) 7 times, p7, k1, p1; rep from * to end.

Row 17 * P1, k9, p1, (k1, p1) 6 times, k9; rep from * to last st, p1.

Row 18 As row 16.

Row 19 As row 15.

Rows 20 to 32 Work from row 14 back to row 2.

Repeat these 32 rows.

Block Quilting

Multiple of 14 sts.

Row 1 (RS) * K4, p6, k4; rep from * to end.

Row 2 Purl.

Rows 3 and 4 Repeat rows 1 and 2 once more.

Row 5 As row 1.

Row 6 * P3, k2, p4, k2, p3; rep from * to end.

Row 7 * K2, p2, k6, p2, k2; rep from * to end.

Row 8 * P1, k2, p8, k2, p1; rep from * to end.

Row 9 * P2, k10, p2; rep from * to end.

Row 10 As row 8.

Row 11 As row 7.

Row 12 As row 6.

Repeat these 12 rows.

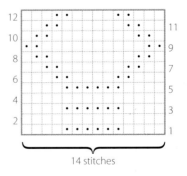

14 stitches

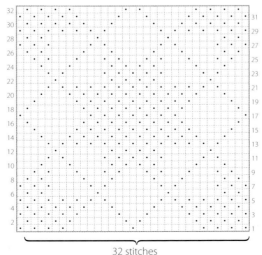

32 stitches

KEY

- · p on RS rows, k on WS rows
- ☐ k on RS rows, p on WS rows

GANSEY PATTERNS

Moss Stitch Ladder

Panel of 5 sts.
Row 1 (RS) P1, (k1, p1) twice.
Row 2 K5.
Repeat these 2 rows.

Two Stitch Ladder

Panel of 8 sts.
Row 1 (RS) P1, k1, p1, k2, p1, k1, p1.
Row 2 K1, p1, k1, p2, k1, p1, k1.
Row 3 P1, k1, p4, k1, p1.
Row 4 K1, p1, k4, p1, k1.
Repeat these 4 rows.

Ladder Stitch

Panel of 10 sts.
Row 1 (RS) P1, k8, p1.
Row 2 K1, p8, k1.
Row 3 P10.
Row 4 As row 2.
Repeat these 4 rows.

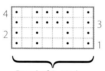

Panel of 5 stitches

Panel of 8 stitches

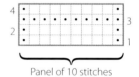

Panel of 10 stitches

KEY

•   p on RS rows, k on WS rows
☐   k on RS rows, p on WS rows

Using gansey patterns

Gansey, Guernsey and Jersey are all names for the traditional sweater worn by fishermen of the British Isles. The stitches are worked in panels, either beginning above the rib or halfway up the body to form a yoke.

Simple ganseys have a repeat pattern of one wide panel, such as Inverness Diamonds (page 21), and one narrow panel, such as Two Stitch Ladder (above).

More complicated patterns can be made by adding more narrow and wide panels to the repeat. Often ganseys will have a panel of a single four stitch cable to add more texture.

Patterns like Anchor (page 19), Tree (page 20) and Humber Star (page 21) can be separated by ridges of reverse stockinette (stocking) stitch to form squares.

GANSEY PATTERNS

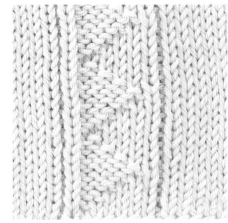

Anchor

Panel of 17 sts.

Row 1 (RS) K8, p1, k8.
Row 2 P7, k1, p1, k1, p7.
Row 3 K6, (p1, k1) twice, p1, k6.
Row 4 (P5, k1) twice, p5.
Row 5 K4, (p1, k3) twice, p1, k4.
Row 6 P3, k1, p9, k1, p3.
Row 7 K2, (p1, k5) twice, p1, k2.
Row 8 (P1, k1) twice, p9, (k1, p1) twice.
Row 9 K2, (p1, k5) twice, p1, k2.
Row 10 P1, k1, p13, k1, p1.
Row 11 K8, p1, k8.
Row 12 Purl.
Rows 13 and 14 Repeat rows 11 and 12 once more.
Row 15 K4, (p1, k1) 4 times, p1, k4.
Row 16 Purl.
Row 17 As row 1.
Row 18 As row 2.
Row 19 As row 1.
Row 20 Purl.
Row 21 Knit.
Row 22 Purl.
Repeat these 22 rows or work rows 1 to 20 for a single motif.

Flags

Panel of 7 sts.

Row 1 (RS) K5, p1, k1.
Row 2 P1, k2, p4.
Row 3 K3, p3, k1.
Row 4 P1, k4, p2.
Row 5 K1, p5, k1.
Row 6 As row 4.
Row 7 As row 3.
Row 8 As row 2.
Repeat these 8 rows.

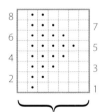

Panel of 7 stitches

Lightning

Panel of 8 sts.

Row 1 (RS) K1, p2, k5.
Row 2 P4, k2, p2.
Row 3 K3, p2, k3.
Row 4 P2, k2, p4.
Row 5 K5, p2, k1.
Row 6 As row 4.
Row 7 As row 3.
Row 8 As row 2.
Repeat these 8 rows.

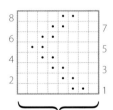

Panel of 8 stitches

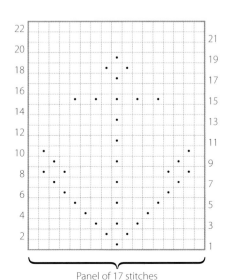

Panel of 17 stitches

KEY

- · p on RS rows, k on WS rows
- ☐ k on RS rows, p on WS rows

GANSEY PATTERNS

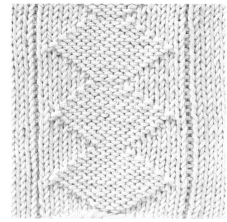
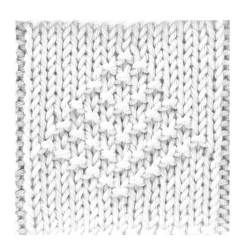

Marriage Lines

Panel of 11 sts.
Row 1 (RS) (K1, p1) twice, k7.
Row 2 P6, k1, p1, k1, p2.
Row 3 K3, p1, k1, p1, k5.
Row 4 P4, k1, p1, k1, p4.
Row 5 K5, p1, k1, p1, k3.
Row 6 P2, k1, p1, k1, p6.
Row 7 K7, (p1, k1) twice.
Row 8 As row 6.
Row 9 As row 5.
Row 10 As row 4.
Row 11 As row 3.
Row 12 As row 2.
Repeat these 12 rows.

Full Diamonds

Panel of 15 sts.
Row 1 (RS) K6, p3, k6.
Row 2 P5, k5, p5.
Row 3 K4, p7, k4.
Row 4 P3, k9, p3.
Row 5 K2, p11, k2.
Row 6 P1, k13, p1.
Row 7 As row 5.
Row 8 As row 4.
Row 9 As row 3.
Row 10 As row 2.
Repeat these 10 rows.

Tree

Panel of 13 sts.
Row 1 (RS) K6, p1, k6.
Row 2 P5, k1, p1, k1, p5.
Row 3 K4, p1, k3, p1, k4.
Row 4 P3, (k1, p2) twice, k1, p3.
Row 5 (K2, p1) twice, k1, (p1, k2) twice.
Row 6 P1, k1, p2, k1, p3, k1, p2, k1, p1.
Row 7 K3, (p1, k2) twice, p1, k3.
Row 8 (P2, k1) twice, p1, (k1, p2) twice.
Row 9 As row 3.
Row 10 As row 4.
Row 11 K5, p1, k1, p1, k5.
Row 12 P4, k1, p3, k1, p4.
Row 13 As row 1.
Row 14 As row 2.
Row 15 As row 1.
Row 16 Purl.
Row 17 Knit.
Row 18 Purl.
Repeat these 18 rows or work rows 1 to 16 for a single motif.

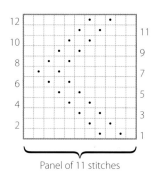

Panel of 11 stitches

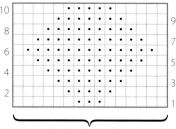

Panel of 15 stitches

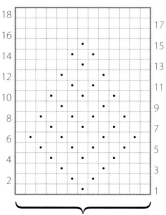

Panel of 13 stitches

KEY

- · p on RS rows, k on WS rows
- ☐ k on RS rows, p on WS rows

GANSEY PATTERNS

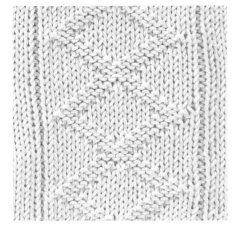

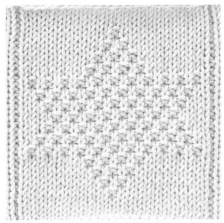

Inverness Diamonds

Panel of 17 sts.
Row 1 (RS) K7, p3, k7.
Row 2 P6, k5, p6.
Row 3 K5, p3, k1, p3, k5.
Row 4 P4, k3, p3, k3, p4.
Row 5 K3, p3, k5, p3, k3.
Row 6 P2, k3, p7, k3, p2.
Row 7 K1, p3, k9, p3, k1.
Rows 8 to 12 Work from row 6
back to row 2.
Repeat these 12 rows.

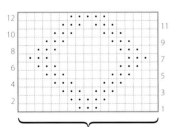

Panel of 17 stitches

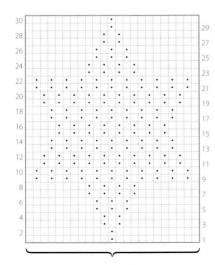

Panel of 23 stitches

Humber Star

Panel of 23 sts.
Row 1 (RS) K11, p1, k11.
Row 2 P11, k1, p11.
Row 3 K10, p1, k1, p1, k10.
Row 4 P10, k1, k1, k1, p10.
Row 5 K9, p1, (k1, p1) twice, k9.
Row 6 P9, k1, (p1, k1) twice, p9.
Row 7 K8, p1, (k1, p1) 3 times, k8.
Row 8 P8, k1, (p1, k1) 3 times, p8.
Row 9 K1, (p1, k1) 11 times.
Row 10 P1, (k1, p1) 11 times.
Row 11 K2, p1, (k1, p1) 9 times, k2.
Row 12 P2, k1, (p1, k1) 9 times, p2.
Row 13 K3, p1, (k1, p1) 8 times, k3.
Row 14 P3, k1, (p1, k1) 8 times, p3.
Row 15 K4, p1, (k1, p1) 7 times, k4.
Row 16 P4, k1, (p1, k1) 7 times, p4.
Row 17 As row 13.
Row 18 As row 14.
Row 19 As row 11.
Row 20 As row 12.
Row 21 As row 9.
Row 22 As row 10.
Row 23 As row 7.
Row 24 As row 8.
Row 25 As row 5.
Row 26 As row 6.
Row 27 As row 3.
Row 28 As row 4.
Row 29 As row 1.
Row 30 As row 2.
Repeat these 30 rows.

KEY

- ● p on RS rows, k on WS rows
- ☐ k on RS rows, p on WS rows

Double Moss Stitch Diamond

Panel of 13 sts.
Row 1 (RS) K6, p1, k6.
Row 2 P6, k1, p6.
Row 3 K5, p1, k1, p1, k5.
Row 4 P5, k1, p1, k1, p5.
Row 5 K4, p1, (k1, p1) twice, k4.
Row 6 P4, k1, (p1, k1) twice, p4.
Row 7 K3, p1, (k1, p1) 3 times, k3.
Row 8 P3, k1, (p1, k1) 3 times, p3.
Row 9 K2, p1, k1, p1, k3, p1, k1, p1, k2.
Row 10 P2, k1, p1, k1, p3, k1, p1, k1, p2.
Row 11 (K1, p1) twice, k5, (p1, k1) twice.
Row 12 (P1, k1) twice, p5, (k1, p1) twice.
Row 13 As row 9.
Row 14 As row 10.
Row 15 As row 7.
Row 16 As row 8.
Row 17 As row 5.
Row 18 As row 6.
Row 19 As row 3.
Row 20 As row 4.
Repeat these 20 rows.

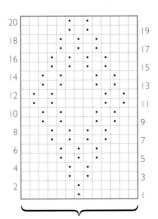

Panel of 13 stitches

TEXTURE STITCHES

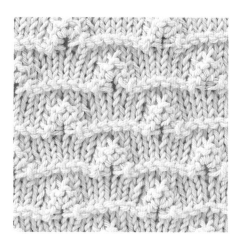

Ruching

On an odd number of stitches.
Row 1 (RS) Knit.
Row 2 Purl.
Rows 3 and 4 Repeat rows 1 and 2 once more.
Row 5 K1, * k into front and back of next st, k1; rep from * to end.
Row 6 Knit.
Row 7 Purl.
Rows 8 to 12 Repeat rows 6 and 7 twice more, then row 6 again.
Row 13 P1, * p2tog, p1; rep from * to end.
Row 14 Knit.
Repeat these 14 rows.

Bubble Pattern

Multiple of 10 sts plus 2.
Row 1 (RS) Knit.
Row 2 Purl.
Row 3 K1, * (k5, turn, p5, turn) 3 times, k10; rep from * to end, ending last rep with k1.
Row 4 Purl.
Row 5 Knit.
Row 6 Purl.
Row 7 K6, * (k5, turn, p5, turn) 3 times, k10; rep from * to last st, k1.
Row 8 Purl.
Repeat these 8 rows.

Textured Picot Stripe

Abbreviation:
M7 – (k1, yfwd, k1, yfwd, k1, yfwd, k1) all into next st.

Multiple of 8 sts plus 5 (stitch count varies).
Row 1 (RS) K2, * M7, k7; rep from * to last 3 sts, M7, k2. 25 sts.
Row 2 Knit.
Row 3 K1, * k2tog, k5, ssk, k5; rep from * to last 10 sts, k2tog, k5, ssk, k1. 22 sts.
Row 4 P1, * ssp, p1, sl 1 wyif, p1, p2tog, p5; rep from * to last 8 sts, ssp, p1, sl 1 wyif, p1, p2tog, p1. 17 sts.
Row 5 K1, * k2tog, sl 1 wyib, ssk, k5; rep from * to last 6 sts, k2tog, sl 1 wyib, ssk, k1. 13 sts.
Row 6 Purl.
Row 7 K2, * k4, M7, k3; rep from * to last 3 sts, k3. 19 sts.
Row 8 Knit.
Row 9 K2, * k3, k2tog, k5, ssk, k2; rep from * to last 3 sts, k3. 17 sts.
Row 10 P3, * p2, ssp, p1, sl 1 wyif, p1, p2tog, p3; rep from * to last 2 sts, p2. 15 sts.
Row 11 K2, * k3, k2tog, sl 1 wyib, ssk, k2; rep from * to last 3 sts, k3. 13 sts.
Row 12 Purl.
Repeat these 12 rows.

TEXTURE STITCHES

Popcorn Pattern

Abbreviations:

MK – purl next 3 sts then pass 2nd and 3rd sts over first st.

MS – (k1, p1, k1) all into next st.

Multiple of 4 sts plus 3 (stitch count varies).

Row 1 (RS) Knit.

Row 2 P1, MS, p1, * p2, MS, p1; rep from * to end. 11 sts.

Row 3 * K1, MK, k2; rep from * to last 5 sts, k1, MK, k1. 7 sts.

Row 4 Purl.

Row 5 Knit.

Row 6 P3, * MS, p3; rep from * to end. 9 sts.

Row 7 * K3, MK; rep from * to last 3 sts, k3. 7 sts.

Row 8 Purl.

Repeat these 8 rows.

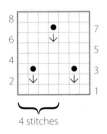

Bramble Stitch

Abbreviation:

MS – (k1, p1, k1) all into next st.

Multiple of 4 sts plus 2.

Row 1 (RS) Purl.

Row 2 K1, * MS, p3tog; rep from * to last st, k1.

Row 3 Purl.

Row 4 K1, * p3tog, MS; rep from * to last st, k1.

Repeat these 4 rows.

Smocking

Abbreviation:

smocking st – insert RH needle from front between 6th and 7th sts, wrap yarn around needle and draw through a loop, sl this loop on to LH needle and k tog with first st on LH needle.

Multiple of 16 sts plus 2.

Row 1 (RS) P2, * k2, p2; rep from * to end.

Row 2 * K2, p2; rep from * to last 2 sts, k2.

Row 3 P2, * smocking st, k1, p2, k2, p2; rep from * to end.

Rows 4 and 6 As row 2.

Row 5 As row 1.

Row 7 P2, k2, p2, * smocking st, k1, p2, k2, p2; rep from * to last 4 sts, k2, p2.

Row 8 As row 2.

Repeat these 8 rows.

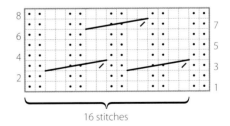

KEY

- MK
- MS
- k on RS rows, p on WS rows

KEY

- p3tog
- MS

- p on RS rows, k on WS rows

KEY

- p on RS rows, k on WS rows
- k on RS rows, p on WS rows
- k2tog

— smocking stitch

TEXTURE STITCHES

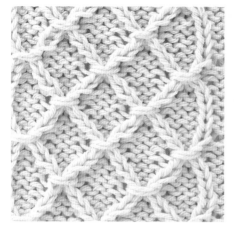

Smocked Honeycomb

Abbreviation:

tie st – sl next 5 sts on to cable needle, wrap yarn around these 5 sts twice, then k1, p3, k1 from cable needle.

Multiple of 16 sts plus 3.
Row 1 (RS) P3, * k1, p3; rep from * to end.
Row 2 * K3, p1; rep from * to last 3 sts, k3.
Row 3 P3, * tie st, p3; rep from * to end.
Rows 4 and 6 As row 2.
Row 5 As row 1.
Row 7 P3, k1, * p3, tie st; rep from * to end, ending last rep with k1, p3.
Row 8 As row 2.
Repeat these 8 rows.

Boxed Bobble

Abbreviation:

MB – k into front, back and front of next st and turn, k3 and turn, p3 and pass 2nd and 3rd sts over first st.

Multiple of 6 sts plus 1.
Row 1 (RS) Purl.
Row 2 and every foll alt row Purl.
Row 3 P1, * k5, p1; rep from * to end.
Row 5 P1, * k2, MB, k2, p1; rep from * to end.
Row 7 As row 3.
Row 8 Purl.
Repeat these 8 rows.

Gooseberry Stitch

Abbreviation:

M5 – (p1, yo, p1, yo, p1) all into next st.

Multiple of 4 sts plus 1.
Row 1 (RS) Knit.
Row 2 K1, * M5, k1; rep from * to end.
Row 3 Purl.
Row 4 K1, * sl 2 wyif, p3tog, psso, k1; rep from * to end.
Row 5 Knit.
Row 6 K1, * k1, M5, k1; rep from * to last st, k1.
Row 7 Purl.
Row 8 K1, * k1, sl 2 wyif, p3tog, psso, k1; rep from * to last st, k1.
Repeat these 8 rows.

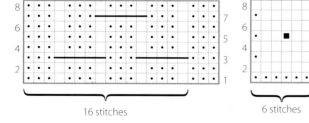

16 stitches

6 stitches

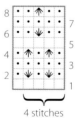

4 stitches

KEY

- • — p on RS rows, k on WS rows
- ☐ — k on RS rows, p on WS rows
- ▬ — tie stitch

KEY

- ■ — MB
- • — p on RS rows, k on WS rows
- ☐ — k on RS rows, p on WS rows

KEY

- ↑ — sl 2 wyif, p3tog, psso
- ↓ — M5
- • — p on RS rows, k on WS rows
- ☐ — k on RS rows, p on WS rows

TEXTURE STITCHES

Dimple Stitch

Abbreviation:

gathering st – take yarn to back of work as though to knit, insert needle from below under 3 strands, k the next st, bring the st out under the strands.

Multiple of 6 sts plus 5.
Row 1 (RS) Knit.
Row 2 P1, * sl 3 wyif, p3; rep from * to end, ending last rep with p1.
Row 3 K1, * sl 3 wyib, k3; rep from * to end, ending last rep with k1.
Row 4 As row 2.
Rows 5 and 7 Knit.
Row 6 Purl.
Row 8 P2, * gathering st, p5; rep from * to end, ending last rep with p2.
Row 9 Knit.
Row 10 P1, * p3, sl 3 wyif; rep from * to last 4 sts, p4.
Row 11 K4, * sl 3 wyif, k3; rep from * to last st, k1.
Row 12 As row 10.
Rows 13 and 15 Knit.
Row 14 Purl.
Row 16 P5, * gathering st, p5; rep from * to end.
Repeat these 16 rows.

Bobble Circle Pattern

Abbreviation:

MS – (k1, p1, k1) all into next st.

Multiple of 12 sts plus 3.
Row 1 (RS) Knit.
Row 2 * P6, MS, p1, MS, p3; rep from * to last 3 sts, p3.
Row 3 K3, * k3, p3, k1, p3, k6; rep from * to end.
Row 4 * P4, MS, (p1, p3tog) twice, p1, MS, p1; rep from * to last 3 sts, p3.
Row 5 K3, * k1, p3, k5, p3, k4; rep from * to end.
Row 6 * P3, MS, p3tog, p5, p3tog, MS; rep from * to last 3 sts, p3.
Row 7 K3, * p3, k7, p3, k3; rep from * to end.
Row 8 * P3, p3tog, p7, p3tog; rep from * to last 3 sts, p3.
Row 9 Knit.
Row 10 * P3, MS, p7, MS; rep from * to last 3 sts, p3.
Row 11 As row 7.
Row 12 * P3, p3tog, MS, p5; MS, p3tog; rep from * to last 3 sts, p3.
Row 13 As row 5.
Row 14 * P4, p3tog, (p1, MS) twice, p1, p3tog, p1; rep from * to last 3 sts, p3.
Row 15 As row 3.
Row 16 * P6, p3tog, p1, p3tog, p3; rep from * to last 3 sts, p3.
Row 17 Knit.
Row 18 Purl.
Repeat these 18 rows.

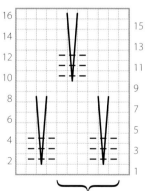

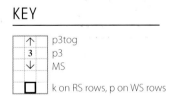

KEY

(gathering symbol)	gathering stitch
–	slip stitch
☐	k on RS rows, p on WS rows

6 stitches

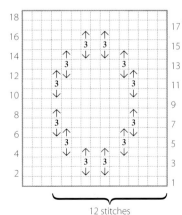

12 stitches

KEY

↑	p3tog
3	p3
↓	MS
☐	k on RS rows, p on WS rows

TEXTURE STITCHES

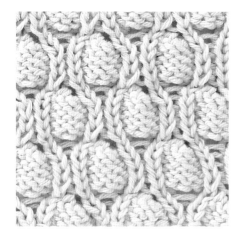

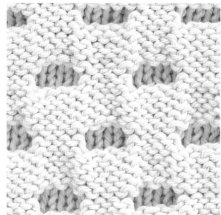

Cocoon Stitch

Abbreviation:

M5 – (p1, yo, p1, yo, p1) all into next st.

Multiple of 8 sts plus 7.
Row 1 (RS) * K1, p5, k1, p1; rep from * to last 7 sts, k1, p5, k1.
Row 2 P1, sl 2 wyif, p3tog, psso, p1, * M5, p1, sl 2 wyif, p3tog, psso, p1; rep from * to end.
Rows 3, 5 and 7 * K1, p1, k1, p5; rep from * to last 3 sts, k1, p1, k1.
Rows 4 and 6 P1, k1, p1, * k5, p1, k1, p1; rep from * to end.
Row 8 P1, M5, p1, * sl 2 wyif, p3tog, psso, p1, M5, p1; rep from * to end.
Row 9 As row 1.
Row 10 P1, k5, p1, * k1, p1, k5, p1; rep from * to end.
Row 11 As row 1.
Row 12 As row 10.
Repeat these 12 rows.

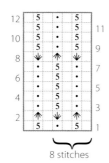

26

Blind Buttonhole Stitch

Multiple of 8 sts plus 6.
Row 1 (WS) Knit.
Row 2 Purl.
Rep these 2 rows once more then row 1 again.
Row 6 K1, * sl 4 wyib, k4; rep from * to last 5 sts, sl 4 wyib, k1.
Row 7 P1, sl 4 wyif, * p4, sl 4 wyif; rep from * to last st, p1.
Rep these 2 rows once more then row 6 again.
Row 11 Knit.
Row 12 Purl.
Rep these 2 rows once more then row 11 again.
Row 16 K5, * sl 4 wyib, k4; rep from * to last st, k1.
Row 17 P5, * sl 4 wyif, p4; rep from * to last st, p1.
Rep these 2 rows once more.
Row 20 As row 16.
Repeat these 20 rows.

Bobble Diamonds

Abbreviation:

MS – (k1, p1, k1) all into next st.

Multiple of 7 sts plus 1.
Row 1 (RS) Knit.
Row 2 P1, * p3, MS, p3; rep from * to end.
Row 3 * K3, p3, k3; rep from * to last st, k1.
Row 4 P1, * p2, MS, p3tog, MS, p2; rep from * to end.
Row 5 * K2, p3, k1, p3, k2; rep from * to last st, k1.
Row 6 P1, * p1, (MS, p3tog) twice, MS, p1; rep from * to end.
Row 7 * (K1, p3) 3 times, k1; rep from * last st, k1.
Row 8 P1, * p1, (p3tog, MS) twice, p3tog, p1; rep from * to end.
Row 9 * K2, p3, k1, p3, k2; rep from * to last st, k1.
Row 10 P1, * p2, p3tog, MS, p3tog, p2; rep from * to end.
Row 11 * K3, p3, k3; rep from * to last st, k1.
Row 12 P1, * p3, p3tog, p3; rep from * to end.
Row 13 Knit.
Row 14 Purl.
Repeat these 14 rows.

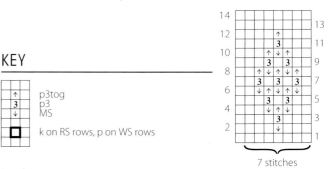

TEXTURE STITCHES

Large Leaf Pattern

Multiple of 13 sts.
Row 1 (RS) * K4, k2tog, (k1, yo, k1) into next st, ssk, k4; rep from * to end.
Row 2 * K4, p5, k4; rep from * to end.
Row 3 * K3, k2tog, (k1, yo) twice, k1, ssk, k3; rep from * to end.
Row 4 * K3, p7, k3; rep from * to end.
Row 5 * K2, k2tog, k2, yo, k1, yo, k2, ssk, k2; rep from * to end.
Row 6 * K2, p9, k2; rep from * to end.
Row 7 * K1, k2tog, k3, yo, k1, yo, k3, ssk, k1; rep from * to end.
Row 8 * K1, p11, k1; rep from * to end.
Row 9 * K1, ssk, k2, yo, k3, yo, k2, k2tog, k1; rep from * to end.
Row 10 As row 8.
Row 11 * K1, yo, ssk, k2, yo, sk2po, yo, k2, k2tog, yo, k1; rep from * to end.
Row 12 As row 6.
Row 13 * K2, yo, ssk, k5, k2tog, yo, k2; rep from * to end.
Row 14 As row 4.
Row 15 * K3, yo, ssk, k3, k2tog, yo, k3; rep from * to end.
Row 16 As row 2.
Row 17 * K4, yo, ssk, k1, k2tog, yo, k4; rep from * to end.
Row 18 * K5, p3, k5; rep from * to end.
Row 19 * K5, yo, sl2tog-k1-psso, yo, k5; rep from * to end.
Row 20 Knit.
Repeat these 20 rows.

Lamb's Tails

Multiple of 4 sts plus 1.
Row 1 (RS) Knit.
Row 2 Knit.
Row 3 * K3, cast on 4 sts, then bind off these 4 sts; rep from * to last st, k1.
Row 4 K1, * p1, k3; rep from * to end.
Row 5 Knit.
Row 6 Knit.
Row 7 K1, * cast on 4 sts, then bind off these 4 sts, k3; rep from * to end.
Row 8 * K3, p1; rep from * to last st, k1.
Repeat these 8 rows.

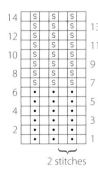

4 stitches

KEY

	cast on and bind off 4 sts
·	p on RS rows, k on WS rows
☐	k on RS rows, p on WS rows

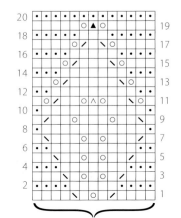

13 stitches

Tuck Rows

Multiple of 2 sts plus 1.
Row 1 (RS) K1, * p1, k1; rep from * to end.
Row 2 P1, * k1, p1; rep from * to end.
Rep rows 1 and 2 twice more.
Row 7 K1, * slip 1 st purlwise wyif of st, k1; rep from * to end.
Row 8 P1, * slip 1 st purlwise wyib of st, p1; rep from * to end.
Rep rows 7 and 8 three times more.
Repeat these 14 rows.

2 stitches

KEY

s	slip st purlwise
·	p on RS rows, k on WS rows
☐	k on RS rows, p on WS rows

KEY

O	yo
/	k2tog
\	ssk
∧	sk2po
▲	sl2tog-k1-psso
·	p on RS rows, k on WS rows
☐	k on RS rows, p on WS rows

RIB STITCHES

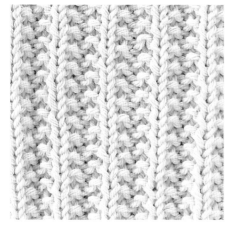

Mistake Rib

Multiple of 4 sts plus 3.
Row 1 * K2, p2; rep from * to last 3 sts, k2, p1.
Repeat this row.

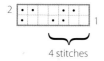

4 stitches

KEY

·	p on RS rows, k on WS rows
☐	k on RS rows, p on WS rows

Rick Rack Rib

Abbreviations:

twist k – take RH needle behind first st and k into back of second st, k first st, slip both sts off LH needle.
twist p – with yarn in front, miss first st and p into second st, p first st, sl both sts off LH needle together.

Multiple of 5 sts plus 1.
Row 1 (RS) K1, * p1, twist k, p1, k1; rep from * to end.
Row 2 * P1, k1, twist p, k1; rep from * to last st, p1.
Repeat these 2 rows.

5 stitches

KEY

✕✕	twist k
✕✕	twist p
·	p on RS rows, k on WS rows
☐	k on RS rows, p on WS rows

Openwork Rib

Multiple of 5 sts plus 2.
Row 1 (RS) P2, * k1, yo, ssk, p2; rep from * to end.
Row 2 * K2, p3; rep from * to last 2 sts, k2.
Row 3 P2, * k2tog, yo, k1, p2; rep from * to end.
Row 4 As row 2.
Repeat these 4 rows.

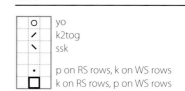

5 stitches

KEY

o	yo
╱	k2tog
╲	ssk
·	p on RS rows, k on WS rows
☐	k on RS rows, p on WS rows

RIB STITCHES

Brioche Stitch

Even number of sts.
Foundation row * Yo, sl 1 wyib, k1; rep from * to end.
Row 1 * Yo, sl 1 wyib, k2tog (sl st and yo of previous row); rep from * to end.
Repeat row 1.

Aran Rib 1

Abbreviation:
Cr3L – slip 1 st on to cable needle at front, k1 tbl, p1, then k1 tbl from cable needle.

Multiple of 8 sts plus 3.
Row 1 (RS) * K3, (p1, k1 tbl) twice, p1; rep from * to last 3 sts, k3.
Row 2 P3, * (k1, p1 tbl) twice, k1; rep from * to end.
Row 3 * K3, p1, Cr3L, p1; rep from * to last 3 sts, k3.
Row 5 As row 1.
Row 6 As row 2.
Repeat these 6 rows.

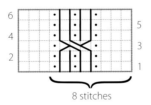

8 stitches

KEY

Cr3L

· p on RS rows, k on WS rows
☐ k on RS rows, p on WS rows

Aran Rib 2

Abbreviations:
Cr2L – slip 1 st on to cable needle at front, p1, k1 tbl from cable needle.
Cr2R – slip 1 st on to cable needle at back, k1 tbl, p1 from cable needle.

Multiple of 7 sts plus 4.
Row 1 (RS) * K4, Cr2L, p1; rep from * to last 4 sts, k4.
Row 2 P4, * k1, p1 tbl, k1, p4; rep from * to end.
Row 3 * K4, p1, Cr2L; rep from * to last 4 sts, k4.
Row 4 P4, * p1 tbl, k2, p4; rep from * to end.
Row 5 * K4, p1, Cr2R; rep from * to last 4 sts, k4.
Row 6 As row 2.
Row 7 * K4, Cr2R, p1; rep from * to last 4 sts, k4.
Row 8 P4, * k2, p1 tbl, p4; rep from * to end.
Repeat these 8 rows.

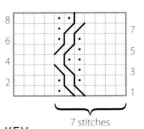

7 stitches

KEY

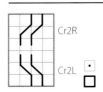

Cr2R

Cr2L

· p on RS rows, k on WS rows
☐ k on RS rows, p on WS rows

RIB STITCHES

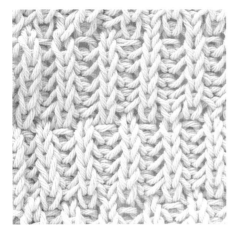

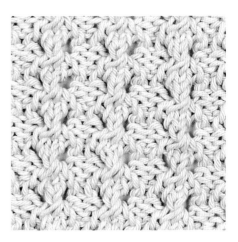

Broken Fisherman's Rib

Multiple of 2 sts

Foundation Row (WS) Purl.

Row 1 * P1, insert needle into the next st on the row below and knit it, letting the st on the needle unravel; rep from * to last 2 sts, p2.

Repeat row 1 ten times more.

Row 12 Purl.

Row 13 P2, * insert needle into the next st on the row below and knit it, letting the st on the needle unravel, p1; rep from * to end.

Repeat row 13 ten times more.

Row 24 Purl.

Repeat these 24 rows.

Fisherman's Rib

Multiple of 2 sts.

Foundation Row (WS) Purl.

Row 1 * P1, insert needle into the next st on the row below and knit it, letting the st on the needle unravel; rep from * to last 2 sts, p2.

Repeat this row.

Puff Rib

Multiple of 3 sts plus 2 (stitch count varies).

Foundation Row (WS) P2, k1, p2.

Row 1 (RS) P2, * yo, k1, yo, p2; rep from * to end. 7 sts.

Row 2 K2, * p3, k2; rep from * to end.

Row 3 P2, * k3, p2; rep from * to end.

Row 4 K2, * p3tog, k2; rep from * to end. 5 sts.

Repeat these 4 rows.

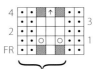

5 stitches

KEY

o yo
↑ p3tog

· p on RS rows, k on WS rows
□ k on RS rows, p on WS rows
   no stitch

RIB STITCHES

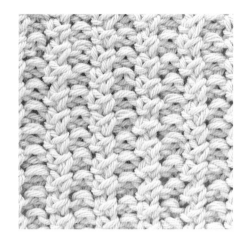

Blanket Rib

Multiple of 2 sts plus 1 (stitch count varies).
Row 1 Kf&b into each st. 6 sts.
Row 2 K2tog, * p2tog, k2tog; rep from * to end. 3 sts.
Repeat these 2 rows.

Harris Tweed Rib

Multiple of 4 sts plus 2.
Row 1 K2, * p2, k2; rep from * to end.
Row 2 P2, * k2, p2; rep from * to end.
Row 3 Knit.
Row 4 Purl.
Row 5 As row 1.
Row 6 As row 2.
Row 7 Purl.
Row 8 Knit.
Repeat these 8 rows.

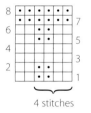

4 stitches

Broken Rib

Multiple of 2 sts plus 1.
Row 1 (RS) Knit.
Row 2 P1, * k1, p1; rep from * to end.
Repeat these 2 rows.

KEY

p on RS rows, k on WS rows
k on RS rows, p on WS rows

CABLE STITCHES

Four Stitch Cable
(crossed every 4th row)

Abbreviations:

C4F – sl 2 sts on to cable needle at front, k2, k2 from cable needle.

Panel of 4 sts on rev st st.
Row 1 (RS) K4.
Row 2 P4.
Row 3 C4F.
Row 4 P4.
Repeat these 4 rows.

Four Stitch Cable
(crossed every 6th row)

Abbreviation:

C4F – sl 2 sts on to cable needle at front, k2, k2 from cable needle.

Panel of 4 sts on rev st st.
Rows 1 and 3 (RS) K4.
Rows 2 and 4 P4.
Row 5 C4F.
Row 6 P4.
Repeat these 6 rows.

To cross the cable to the right work C4B instead of C4F.
Abbreviation:
C4B – sl 2 sts on to cable needle at back, k2, k2 from cable needle.

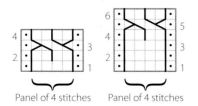

Panel of 4 stitches   Panel of 4 stitches

Six Stitch Cable
(crossed every 6th row)

Abbreviations:

C6F – sl 3 sts on to cable needle at front, k3, k3 from cable needle.
Panel of 6 sts on rev st st.
Rows 1 and 3 (RS) K6.
Row 2 and every foll WS row P6.
Row 5 C6F.
Row 6 P6.
Repeat these 6 rows.

Six Stitch Cable
(crossed every 8th row)

Abbreviation:

C6F – sl 3 sts on to cable needle at front, k3, k3 from cable needle.

Panel of 6 sts on rev st st.
Rows 1, 3 and 5 (RS) K6.
Row 2 and every foll WS row P6.
Row 7 C6F.
Row 8 P6.
Repeat these 8 rows.

To cross the cable to the right work C6B instead of C6F.
Abbreviation:
C6B – sl 3 sts on to cable needle at back, k3, k3 from cable needle.

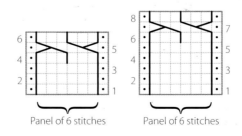

Panel of 6 stitches   Panel of 6 stitches

Four Stitch Wave Cable

Abbreviations:

C4F – sl 2 sts on to cable needle at front, k2, k2 from cable needle.
C4B – sl 2 sts on to cable needle at back, k2, k2 from cable needle.

Panel of 4 sts on rev st st.
Rows 1 and 5 (RS) K4.
Row 2 and every foll WS row P4.
Row 3 C4F.
Row 7 C4B.
Row 8 P4.
Repeat these 8 rows.

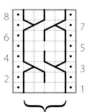

Panel of 4 stitches

KEY

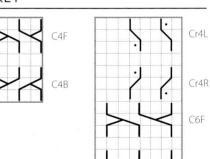

C4F
C4B
Cr4L
Cr4R
C6F
C6B

■ MB
· p on RS rows, k on WS rows
□ k on RS rows, p on WS rows

CABLE STITCHES

Ensign's Braid

Abbreviations:

Cr4L – sl 3 sts on to cable needle at front, p1, k3 from cable needle.
Cr4R – sl 1 st on to cable needle at back, k3, p1 from cable needle.
C6F – sl 3 sts on to cable needle at front, k3, k3 from cable needle.
C6B – sl 3 sts on to cable needle at back, k3, k3 from cable needle.

Panel of 20 sts on rev st st.
Row 1 (RS) K3, p4, C6B, p4, k3.
Row 2 and every foll WS row K all k sts and p all p sts.
Row 3 (Cr4L, p2, Cr4R) twice.
Row 5 (P1, Cr4L, Cr4R, p1) twice.
Row 7 P2, C6F, p4, C6B, p2.
Row 9 (P1, Cr4R, Cr4L, p1) twice.
Row 11 (Cr4R, p2, Cr4L) twice.
Row 13 K3, p4, C6F, p4, k3.
Row 15 As row 3.
Row 17 As row 5.
Row 19 P2, C6B, p4, C6F, p2.
Row 21 As row 9.
Row 23 As row 11.
Row 24 (P3, k4, p3) twice.
Repeat these 24 rows.

Oxo Cable

Abbreviations:

C4F – sl 2 sts on to cable needle at front, k2, k2 from cable needle.
C4B – sl 2 sts on to cable needle at back, k2, k2 from cable needle.

Panel of 8 sts on rev st st.
Row 1 (RS) K8.
Row 2 P8.
Row 3 C4B, C4F.
Row 4 P8.
Rows 5 to 8 As rows 1 to 4.
Row 9 K8.
Row 10 P8.
Row 11 C4F, C4B.
Row 12 P8.
Rows 13 to 16 As rows 9 to 12.
Repeat these 16 rows.

Medallion Bobble Cable

Abbreviations:

MB – (k1, p1) twice into next st and turn, p4 and turn, k4 and turn, (p2tog) twice and turn, k2tog.
C6F – sl 3 sts on to cable needle at front, k3, k3 from cable needle.
C6B – sl 3 sts on to cable needle at back, k3, k3 from cable needle.

Panel of 15 sts.
Rows 1, 3, 7, 11 and 15 (RS) P1, k13, p1.
Row 2 and every foll WS row K1, p13, k1.
Row 5 P1, C6B, k1, C6F, p1.
Row 9 P1, k6, MB, k6, p1.
Row 13 P1, C6F, k1, C6B, p1.
Row 16 As row 2.
Repeat these 16 rows.

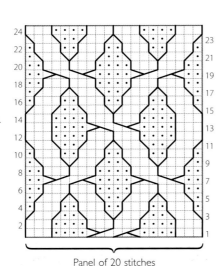

Panel of 20 stitches

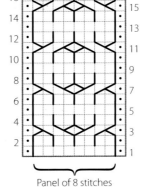

Panel of 8 stitches

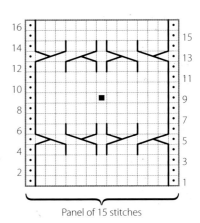

Panel of 15 stitches

CABLE STITCHES

Five Rib Braid

Abbreviations:

C5F – sl 3 sts on to cable needle at front, k2, sl p st back on to LH needle and p it, k2 from cable needle.

C5B – sl 3 sts on to cable needle at back, k2, sl p st back on to LH needle and p it, k2 from cable needle.

Panel of 18 sts on rev st st.
Row 1 (RS) P2, (k2, p1) 5 times, p1.
Row 2 and every foll WS row K2, (p2, k1) 5 times, k1.
Row 3 P2, k2, (p1, C5F) twice, p2.
Row 5 As row 1.
Row 7 P2, (C5B, p1) twice, k2, p2.
Row 8 As row 2.
Repeat these 8 rows.

Celtic Cable

Abbreviations:

Cr3L – sl 2 sts on to cable needle at front, p1, k2 from cable needle.

Cr3R – sl 1 st on to cable needle at back, k2, p1 from cable needle.

Cr4L – sl 2 sts on to cable needle at front, p2, k2 from cable needle.

Cr4R – sl 2 sts on to cable needle at back, k2, p2 from cable needle.

C4F – sl 2 sts on to cable needle at front, k2, k2 from cable needle.

C4B – sl 2 sts on to cable needle at back, k2, k2 from cable needle.

Panel of 24 sts on rev st st.
Row 1 (RS) (P2, C4B, p2) 3 times.
Row 2 and every foll WS row K all k sts and p all p sts.
Row 3 P1, Cr3R, (Cr4L, Cr4R) twice, Cr3L, p1.
Row 5 Cr3R, p1, (p2, C4F, p2) twice, p1, Cr3L.
Row 7 K2, p2, (Cr4R, Cr4L) twice, p2, k2.
Row 9 (K2, p2) twice, p2, C4B, p2, (p2, k2) twice.
Row 11 K2, p2, (Cr4L, Cr4R) twice, p2, k2.
Row 13 Cr3L, p1, (p2, C4F, p2) twice, p1, Cr3R.
Row 15 P1, Cr3L, (Cr4R, Cr4L) twice, Cr3R, p1.
Row 16 (K2, p4, k2) 3 times.
Repeat these 16 rows.

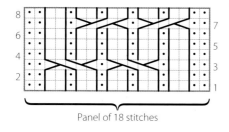

Panel of 18 stitches

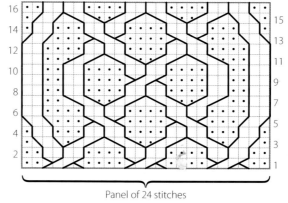

Panel of 24 stitches

Triple Twist Cable

Abbreviations:

Cr4L – sl 2 sts on to cable needle at front, p2, k2 from cable needle.
Cr4R – sl 2 sts on to cable needle at back, k2, p2 from cable needle.
C4F – sl 2 sts on to cable needle at front, k2, k2 from cable needle.
C4B – sl 2 sts on to cable needle at back, k2, k2 from cable needle.

Panel of 24 sts on rev st st.
Row 1 (RS) (P2, C4B, p2) 3 times.
Row 2 and every foll WS row K all k sts and p all p sts.
Row 3 Cr4R, Cr4L, p2, k4, p2, Cr4R, Cr4L.
Row 5 K2, p4, k2, p2, C4B, p2, k2, p4, k2.
Row 7 Cr4L, Cr4R, p2, k4, p2, Cr4L, Cr4R.
Row 9 As row 1.
Row 11 (Cr4R, Cr4L) 3 times.
Row 13 K2, (p4, C4F) twice, p4, k2.
Row 15 (Cr4L, Cr4R) 3 times.
Row 16 (K2, p4, k2) 3 times.
Repeat these 16 rows.

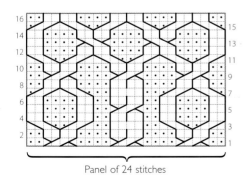

Panel of 24 stitches

Hollow Oak

Abbreviations:

MB – (k1, k1 tbl, k1, k1 tbl, k1) all into next st, pass 2nd, 3rd, 4th and 5th sts over first.
Cr3L – sl 2 sts on to cable needle at front, p1, k2 from cable needle.
Cr3R – sl 1 st on to cable needle at back, k2, p1 from cable needle.
C3F – sl 2 sts on to cable needle at front, k1, k2 from cable needle.
C3B – sl 1 st on to cable needle at back, k2, k1 from cable needle.

Panel of 11 sts on rev st st.
Row 1 (RS) P3, k2, MB, k2, p3.
Rows 2, 4 and 6 K3, p5, k3.
Row 3 P3, MB, k3, MB, p3.
Row 5 As row 1.
Row 7 P2, C3B, p1, C3F, p2.
Row 8 K2, p2, k1, p1, k1, p2, k2.
Row 9 P1, Cr3R, k1, p1, k1, Cr3L, p1.
Row 10 K1, p3, k1, p1, k1, p3, k1.
Row 11 C3B, (p1, k1) twice, p1, C3F.
Row 12 P2, (k1, p1) 4 times, p1.
Row 13 K3, (p1, k1) 3 times, k2.
Row 14 As row 12.
Row 15 Cr3L, (p1, k1) twice, p1, Cr3R.
Row 16 As row 10.
Row 17 P1, Cr3L, k1, p1, k1, Cr3R, p1.
Row 18 As row 8.
Row 19 P2, Cr3L, p1, Cr3R, p2.
Row 20 As row 2.
Repeat these 20 rows.

KEY

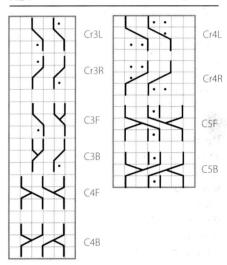

Cr3L
Cr3R
C3F
C3B
C4F
C4B

Cr4L
Cr4R
C5F
C5B

■ MB
· p on RS rows, k on WS rows
□ k on RS rows, p on WS rows

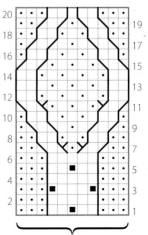

Panel of 11 stitches

CABLE STITCHES

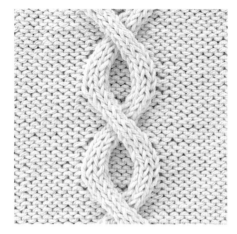

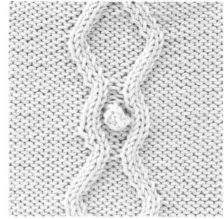

Circle Cable

Abbreviations:

Cr4L – sl 3 sts on to cable needle at front, p1, k3 from cable needle.

Cr4R – sl 1 st on to cable needle at back, k3, p1 from cable needle.

Cr5L – sl 3 sts on to cable needle at front, p2, k3 from cable needle.

Cr5R – sl 2 sts on to cable needle at back, k3, p2 from cable needle.

C6F – sl 3 sts on to cable needle at front, k3, k3 from cable needle.

Panel of 12 sts on rev st st.
Row 1 (RS) P1, Cr5R, Cr5L, p1.
Row 2 and every foll WS row K all k sts and p all p sts.
Row 3 Cr4R, p4, Cr4L.
Row 5 K3, p6, k3.
Row 7 Cr4L, p4, Cr4R.
Row 9 P1, Cr5L, Cr5R, p1.
Row 11 P3, C6F, p3.
Row 12 K3, p6, k3.
Repeat these 12 rows.

Ripple and Rock

Abbreviations:

MB – (k1, yfwd, k1, yfwd, k1) all into next st, turn and p5, turn and k5, turn and p2tog, p1, p2tog, turn and k3tog.

Cr3L – sl 2 sts on to cable needle at front, p1, k2 from cable needle.

Cr3R – sl 1 st on to cable needle at back, k2, p1 from cable needle.

Panel of 13 sts on rev st st.
Row 1 (RS) P3, Cr3R, p1, Cr3L, p3.
Row 2 and every foll WS row K all k sts and p all p sts.
Row 3 P2, Cr3R, p3, Cr3L, p2.
Row 5 P1, Cr3R, p5, Cr3L, p1.
Row 7 Cr3R, p7, Cr3L.
Row 9 Cr3L, p7, Cr3R.
Row 11 P1, Cr3L, p5, Cr3R, p1.
Row 13 P2, Cr3L, p3, Cr3R, p2.
Row 15 P3, Cr3L, p1, Cr3R, p3.
Row 17 As row 1.
Row 19 As row 3.
Row 21 P2, k2, p2, MB, p2, k2, p2.
Row 23 As row 13.
Row 25 As row 15.
Row 26 K4, p2, k1, p2, k4.
Repeat these 26 rows.

Braid Cable

Abbreviations:

Cr3L – sl 2 sts on to cable needle at front, p1, k2 from cable needle.

Cr3R – sl 1 st on to cable needle at back, k2, p1 from cable needle.

C4F – sl 2 sts on to cable needle at front, k2, k2 from cable needle.

C4B – sl 2 sts on to cable needle at back, k2, k2 from cable needle.

Panel of 9 sts on rev st st.
Row 1 (RS) Cr3L, Cr3R, Cr3L.
Row 2 and every foll WS row K all k sts and p all p sts.
Row 3 P1, C4B, p2, k2.
Row 5 Cr3R, Cr3L, Cr3R.
Row 7 K2, p2, C4F, p1.
Row 8 K1, p4, k2, p2.
Repeat these 8 rows.

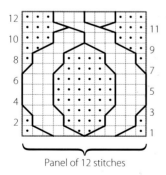

Panel of 12 stitches

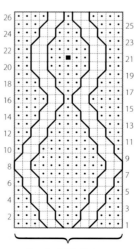

Panel of 13 stitches

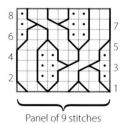

Panel of 9 stitches

CABLE STITCHES

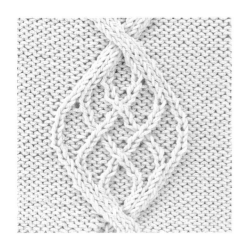

Trellis Diamond

Abbreviations:

Cr2L – sl 1 st on to cable needle at front, p1, k1 from cable needle.

Cr2R – sl 1 st on to cable needle at back, k1, p1 from cable needle.

Cr3L – sl 2 sts on to cable needle at front, p1, k2 from cable needle.

Cr3R – sl 1 st on to cable needle at back, k2, p1 from cable needle.

Cr4L – sl 3 sts on to cable needle at front, p1, k3 from cable needle.

Cr4R – sl 1 st on to cable needle at back, k3, p1 from cable needle.

C2FP – sl 1 st on to cable needle at WS, p1, p1 from cable needle.

C2BP – sl 1 st on to cable needle at RS, p1, p1 from cable needle.

C6F – sl 3 sts on to cable needle at front, k3, k3 from cable needle.

Panel of 18 sts on rev st st.

Row 1 (RS) P5, Cr4R, Cr4L, p5.

Row 2 and every foll WS row except rows 10,14 and 18 K all k sts and p all p sts.

Row 3 P4, Cr4R, p2, Cr4L, p4.

Row 5 P3, Cr3R, k1, p4, k1, Cr3L, p3.

Row 7 P2, Cr3R, p1, Cr2L, p2, Cr2R, p1, Cr3L, p2.

Row 9 P1, Cr2R, k1, p3, Cr2L, Cr2R, p3, k1, Cr2L, p1.

Row 10 (K1, p1) twice, k4, C2FP, k4, (p1, k1) twice.

Row 11 Cr2R, p1, (Cr2L, p2, Cr2R) twice, p1, Cr2L.

Row 13 K1, p3, (Cr2L, Cr2R, p2) twice, p1, k1.

Row 14 P1, (k4, C2BP) twice, k4, p1.

Row 15 K1, p3, (Cr2R, Cr2L, p2) twice, p1, k1.

Row 17 Cr2L, p1, (Cr2R, p2, Cr2L) twice, p1, Cr2R.

Row 18 As row 10.

Row 19 P1, Cr2L, k1, p3, Cr2R, Cr2L, p3, k1, Cr2R, p1.

Row 21 P2, Cr3L, p1, Cr2R, p2, Cr2L, p1, Cr3R, p2.

Row 23 P3, Cr3L, k1, p4, k1, Cr3R, p3.

Row 25 P4, Cr4L, p2, Cr4R, p4.

Row 27 P5, Cr4L, Cr4R, p5.

Row 29 P6, C6F, p6.

Row 30 K6, p6, k6.

Repeat these 30 rows.

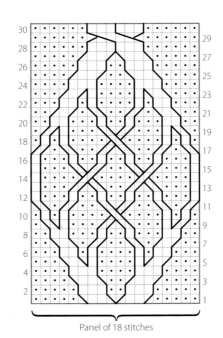

Panel of 18 stitches

KEY

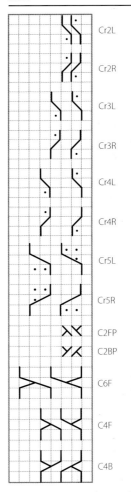

Cr2L
Cr2R
Cr3L
Cr3R
Cr4L
Cr4R
Cr5L
Cr5R
C2FP
C2BP
C6F
C4F
C4B

■ MB

· p on RS rows, k on WS rows

□ k on RS rows, p on WS rows

CABLE STITCHES

Grapes on the Vine

Abbreviations:

MS – (k1, p1, k1) all into next st.
Cr2L – sl 1 st on to cable needle at front, p1, k1 from cable needle.
Cr2R – sl 1 st on to cable needle at back, k1, p1 from cable needle.
Cr3L – sl 2 sts on to cable needle at front, p1, k2 from cable needle.
Cr3R – sl 1 st on to cable needle at back, k2, p1 from cable needle.
Cr4L – sl 2 sts on to cable needle at front, p2, k2 from cable needle.
Cr4R – sl 2 sts on to cable needle at back, k2, p2 from cable needle.

Panel of 14 sts on rev st st (stitch count varies on some rows).

Row 1 (RS) P3, Cr3L, p4, k1, p3.
Rows 2, 4, 16 and 18 K all k sts and p all p sts.
Row 3 P4, Cr4L, p1, Cr2R, p3.
Row 5 P3, k1, p2, Cr4L, p4.
Row 6 K4, p2, k4, MS, k3. 16 sts.
Row 7 P2, (k1, p3) twice, Cr3L, p3.
Row 8 K3, p2, k4, MS, p3tog, MS, k2. 18 sts.
Row 9 P1, (k1, p3) 3 times, Cr3L, p2.
Row 10 K2, p2, k4, MS, (p3tog, MS) twice, k1. 20 sts.
Row 11 (K1, p3) 4 times, k2, p2.
Row 12 K2, p2, k4, p3tog, (MS, p3tog) twice, k1. 18 sts.
Row 13 P1, (k1, p3) 3 times, Cr3R, p2.
Row 14 K3, p2, k4, p3tog, p1, p3tog, k2. 14 sts.
Row 15 P3, k1, p4, Cr3R, p3.
Row 17 P3, Cr2L, p1, Cr4R, p4.

Row 19 P4, Cr4R, p2, k1, p3.
Row 20 K3, MS, k4, p2, k4. 16 sts.
Row 21 P3, Cr3R, (p3, k1) twice, p2.
Row 22 K2, MS, p3tog, MS, k4, p2, k3. 18 sts.
Row 23 P2, Cr3R, (p3, k1) 3 times, p1.
Row 24 K1, MS, (p3tog, MS) twice, k4, p2, k2. 20 sts.
Row 25 P2, k2, (p3, k1) 4 times.
Row 26 K1, p3tog, (MS, p3tog) twice, k4, p2, k2. 18 sts.
Row 27 P2, Cr3L, (p3, k1) 3 times, p1.
Row 28 K2, p3tog, p1, p3tog, k4, p2, k3. 14 sts.
Repeat these 28 rows.

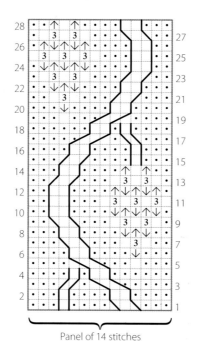

Panel of 14 stitches

KEY

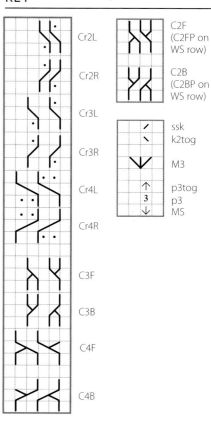

Cr2L
Cr2R
Cr3L
Cr3R
Cr4L
Cr4R
C3F
C3B
C4F
C4B

C2F (C2FP on WS row)
C2B (C2BP on WS row)

ssk
k2tog
M3
p3tog
p3
MS

■ MB
· p on RS rows, k on WS rows
☐ k on RS rows, p on WS rows

CABLE STITCHES

Heart Cable

Abbreviations:

M3 – (k1 tbl, k1) into next st, pick up vertical strand between these 2 sts and k into back of it.

Cr3L – sl 2 sts on to cable needle at front, p1, k2 from cable needle.

Cr3R – sl 1 st on to cable needle at back, k2, p1 from cable needle.

Cr4L – sl 2 sts on to cable needle at front, p2, k2 from cable needle.

Cr4R – sl 2 sts on to cable needle at back, k2, p2 from cable needle.

C3F – sl 2 sts on to cable needle at front, k1, k2 from cable needle.

C3B – sl 1 st on to cable needle at back, k2, k1 from cable needle.

C4F – sl 2 sts on to cable needle at front, k2, k2 from cable needle.

C4B – sl 2 sts on to cable needle at back, k2, k2 from cable needle.

Panel of 21 sts.

Row 1 (RS) P1, k3, (p1, k1) twice, ssk, M3, k2tog, (k1, p1) twice, k3, p1.

Row 2 K1, p2, (k1, p1) 3 times, p3, (p1, k1) 3 times, p2, k1.

Row 3 P1, Cr3L, p1, k1, p1, ssk, k1, M3, k1, k2tog, p1, k1, p1, Cr3R, p1.

Row 4 K2, p3, k1, p1, k1, p5, k1, p1, k1, p3, k2.

Row 5 P2, Cr4L, C4B, p1, C4F, Cr4R, p2.

Row 6 K4, p5, k1, p1, k1, p5, k4.

Row 7 P4, C4B, (p1, k1) twice, p1, C4F, p4.

Row 8 K4, p3, (k1, p1) 4 times, p2, k4.

Row 9 P2, C4B, (p1, k1) 4 times, p1, C4F, p2.

Row 10 K2, p3, (k1, p1) 6 times, p2, k2.

Row 11 P1, C3B, (p1, k1) 6 times, p1, C3F, p1.

Row 12 K1, p2, (k1, p1) 7 times, k1, p2, k1.

Repeat these 12 rows.

Nosegay Pattern

Abbreviations:

MB – (k1, p1) twice into next st and turn, p4 and turn, k4 and turn, (p2tog) twice and turn, k2tog.

Cr2L – sl 1 st on to cable needle at front, p1, k1 from cable needle.

Cr2R – sl 1 st on to cable needle at back, k1, p1 from cable needle.

C2F – sl 1 st on to cable needle at front, k1, k1 from cable needle.

C2B – sl 1 st on to cable needle at back, k1, k1 from cable needle.

C2FP – sl 1 st on to cable needle at WS, p1, p1 from cable needle.

C2BP – sl 1 st on to cable needle at RS, p1, p1 from cable needle.

Panel of 16 sts on rev st st.

Row 1 (RS) P6, C2B, C2F, p6.

Row 2 K5, C2FP, p2, C2BP, k5.

Row 3 P4, Cr2R, C2B, C2F, Cr2L, p4.

Row 4 K3, Cr2L, k1, p4, k1, Cr2R, k3.

Row 5 P2, Cr2R, p1, Cr2R, k2, Cr2L, p1, Cr2L, p2.

Row 6 (K2, p1) twice, k1, p2, k1, (p1, k2) twice.

Row 7 P2, MB, p1, Cr2R, p1, k2, p1, Cr2L, p1, MB, p2.

Row 8 K4, p1, k2, p2, k2, p1, k4.

Row 9 P4, MB, p2, k2, p2, MB, p4.

Row 10 K7, p2, k7

Repeat these 10 rows.

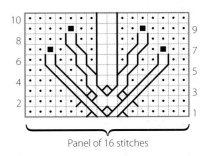

Panel of 16 stitches

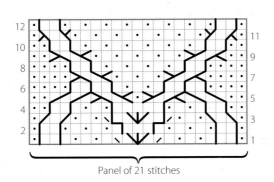

Panel of 21 stitches

CABLE STITCHES

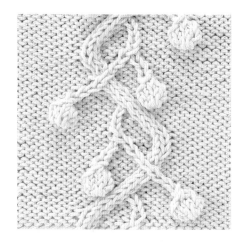

Twisted Vine

Abbreviations:

MB – (k1, p1, k1, p1, k1) all into next st and turn, p5 and turn, k5 and turn, p2tog, p1, p2tog and turn, k3tog. P st above bobble on next row.

Cr2L – sl 1 st on to cable needle at front, p1, k1 from cable needle.

Cr2R – sl 1 st on to cable needle at back, k1, p1 from cable needle.

Cr3L – sl 1 st on to cable needle at front, p2, k1 from cable needle.

Cr3R – sl 2 sts on to cable needle at back, k1, p2 from cable needle.

Cr4L – sl 2 sts on to cable needle at front, p2, k2 from cable needle.

Cr4R – sl 2 sts on to cable needle at back, k2, p2 from cable needle.

C3F – sl 1 st on to cable needle at front, k2, k1 from cable needle.

C3B – sl 2 sts on to cable needle at back, k1, k2 from cable needle.

Panel of 17 sts on rev st st.
Row 1 (RS) P6, k1, p4, Cr4R, p2.
Row 2 and every foll WS row K all k sts and p all p sts.
Row 3 MB, p5, Cr2L, p1, Cr4R, p4.
Row 5 Cr3L, p4, Cr4R, p6.
Row 7 P2, Cr3L, Cr4R, p3, MB, p4.
Row 9 P4, C3F, p4, Cr2R, p4.
Row 11 P2, Cr4R, Cr3L, p1, Cr2R, p5.
Row 13 P2, k2, p4, Cr3L, p6.

Row 15 P2, Cr4L, p4, k1, p6.
Row 17 P4, Cr4L, p1, Cr2R, p5, MB.
Row 19 P6, Cr4L, p4, Cr3R.
Row 21 P4, MB, p3, Cr4L, Cr3R, p2.
Row 23 P4, Cr2L, p4, C3B, p4.
Row 25 P5, Cr2L, p1, Cr3R, Cr4L, p2.
Row 27 P6, Cr3R, p4, k2, p2.
Row 28 K2, p2, k6, p1, k6.
Repeat these 28 rows.

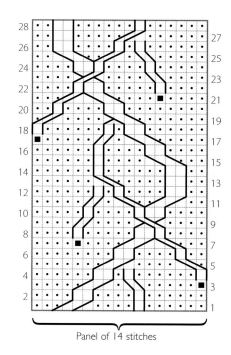

Panel of 14 stitches

KEY

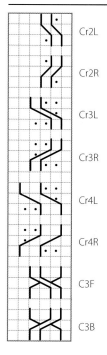

Cr2L
Cr2R
Cr3L
Cr3R
Cr4L
Cr4R
C3F
C3B

■ MB

⊡ p on RS rows, k on WS rows

☐ k on RS rows, p on WS rows

CABLE STITCHES

Framed Cable

Panel of 18 sts.
Row 1 (RS) K4, Cr2R, k6, Cr2L, k4.
Row 2 P5, k1, p6, k1, p5.
Row 3 K3, Cr2R, p1, k6, p1, Cr2L, k3.
Row 4 P4, k2, p6, k2, p4.
Row 5 K2, Cr2R, p2, C6B, p2, Cr2L, k2.
Row 6 P3, k3, p6, k3, p3.
Row 7 K1, Cr2R, p3, k6, p3, Cr2L, k1.
Row 8 P2, k4, p6, k4, p2.
Row 9 K1, C2F, p3, k6, p3, C2B, k1.
Row 10 As row 6.
Row 11 K2, C2F, p2, C6B, p2, C2B, k2.
Row 12 As row 4.
Row 13 K3, C2F, p1, k6, p1, C2B, k3.
Row 14 As row 2.
Row 15 K4, C2F, k6, C2B, k4.
Row 16 P18.
Repeat these 16 rows.

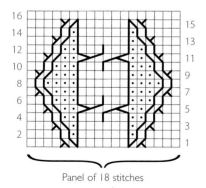

Panel of 18 stitches

Eyelet Cable

Panel of 9 sts.
Row 1 (RS) P2, C5F, p2.
Row 2 K2, p5, k2.
Row 3 P1, C3B, k1, C3F, p1.
Row 4 K1, p7, k1.
Row 5 P1, k2, yo, sl2tog-k1-p2sso, yo, k2, p1.
Repeat rows 4 and 5 three times more.
Row 12 As row 4.
Row 13 P1, k7, p1.
Row 14 As row 4.
Row 15 P1, Cr3L, k1, Cr3R, p1.
Row 16 As row 2.
Repeat these 16 rows.

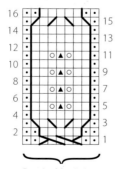

Panel of 9 stitches

Abbreviations:

Cr2R – sl 1 st on to cable needle at back, k1, then p1 from cable needle.
Cr2L – sl 1 st on to cable needle at front, p1, then k1 from cable needle.
C6B – sl 3 sts on to cable needle at back, k3, then k3 from cable needle.
C2F – sl 1 st on to cable needle at front, k1, then k1 from cable needle.
C2B – sl 1 st on to cable needle at back, k1, k1 from cable needle.
C5F – sl 2 sts on to cable needle at front, k3, then k2 from cable needle.
C3B – sl 1 st on to cable needle at back, k2, then k1 from cable needle.
C3F – sl 2 sts on to cable needle at front, k1, then k2 from cable needle.
Cr3L – sl 2 sts on to cable needle at front, p1, then k2 from cable needle.
Cr3R – sl 1 st on to cable needle at back, k2, then p1 from cable needle.

KEY

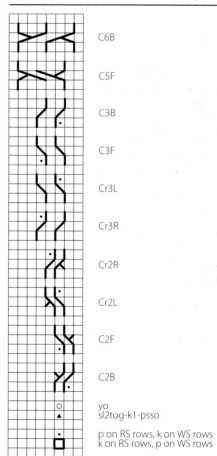

C6B

C5F

C3B

C3F

Cr3L

Cr3R

Cr2R

Cr2L

C2F

C2B

yo
sl2tog-k1-psso

p on RS rows, k on WS rows
k on RS rows, p on WS rows

CABLE STITCHES

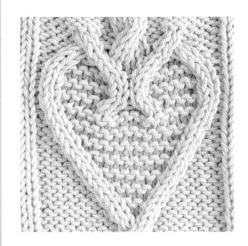

Heart Cable

Abbreviations:

C4F – sl 2 sts on to cable needle at front, k2, then k2 from cable needle.

C4B – sl 2 sts on to cable needle at back, k2, then k2 from cable needle.

C3F – sl 2 sts on to cable needle at front, k1, then k2 from cable needle.

C3B – sl 1 st on to cable needle at back, k2, then k1 from cable needle.

C4B – sl 2 sts on to cable needle at back, k2, then k2 from cable needle.

Cr4R – sl 2 sts on to cable needle at back, k2, then p2 from cable needle.

Cr4L – sl 2 sts on to cable needle at front, p2, then k2 from cable needle.

Cr3L – sl 2 sts on to cable needle at front, p1, then k2 from cable needle.

Cr3R – sl 1 st on to cable needle at back, k2, then p1 from cable needle.

Panel of 22 sts.
Foundation Row (WS) K9, p4, k9.
Row 1 P9, C4B, p9.
Row 2 K9, p4, k9.
Row 3 P9, k4, p9.
Row 4 As row 2.
Row 5 As row 1.
Row 6 As row 2.
Row 7 P8, C3B, C3F, p8.
Row 8 K8, p2, k2, p2, k8.
Row 9 P7, C3B, k2, C3F, p7.
Row 10 K7, p2, k4, p2, k7.
Row 11 P6, C3B, k4, C3F, p6.
Row 12 (K6, p2) twice, k6.
Row 13 P5, C3B, k6, C3F, p5.
Row 14 K5, p2, k8, p2, k5.
Row 15 P4, C3B, k8, C3F, p4.

Row 16 K4, p2, k10, p2, k4.
Row 17 P3, C3B, k10, C3F, p3.
Row 18 K3, p2, k12, p2, k3.
Row 19 P2, C3B, k12, C3F, p2.
Row 20 K2, p2, k14, p2, k2.
Row 21 P1, C3B, k14, C3F, p1.
Row 22 K1, (p2, k4) 3 times, p2, k1.
Row 23 P1, k6, C4F, C4B, k6, p1.
Row 24 K1, p2, k6, p4, k6, p2, k1.
Row 25 P1, k20, p1.
Row 26 As row 24.
Row 27 P1, (C3F, k4, C3B) twice, p1.
Row 28 K2, p2, k4, p6, k4, p2, k2.
Row 29 P2, Cr4L, C4B, k2, C4F, Cr4R, p2.
Row 30 K4, p4, k1, p4, k1, p4, k4.
Row 31 P4, Cr4R, p1, k4, p1, Cr4L, p4.
Row 32 K9, p4, k9.
Repeat these 32 rows.

KEY

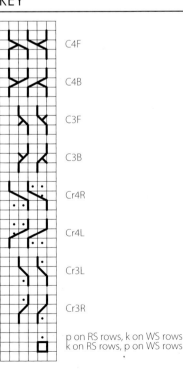

C4F

C4B

C3F

C3B

Cr4R

Cr4L

Cr3L

Cr3R

p on RS rows, k on WS rows
k on RS rows, p on WS rows

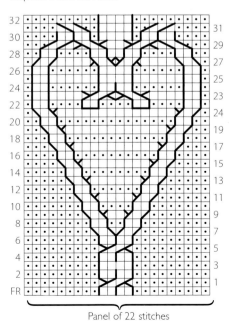

Panel of 22 stitches

CABLE STITCHES

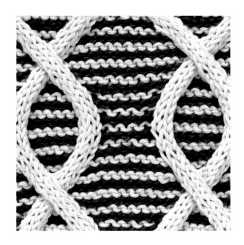

Two-Colour Cable

Abbreviations:

C6F – sl 3 sts on to cable needle at front, k3, then k3 from cable needle.

C5B – sl 2 sts on to cable needle at back, k3, then k2 from cable needle.

C5F – sl 3 sts on to cable needle at front, k2, then k3 from cable needle.

C4B – sl 1 st on to cable needle at back, k3, then k1 from cable needle.

C4F – sl 3 sts on to cable needle at front, k1, then k3 from cable needle.

Panel of 20 sts.

Use 2 colours A and B

Row 1 (RS) Using A, k7, C6F, k7.

Row 2 Using A, k7, p6, k7.

Row 3 Using B, k7, slip 6 sts purlwise with yarn at WS, k7.

Row 4 Using B, k7, slip 6 sts purlwise with yarn at WS, k7.

Row 5 Using A, k5, C5B, C5F, k5.

Row 6 Using A, k5, p3, k4, p3, k5.

Row 7 Using B, k5, slip 3 sts purlwise with yarn at WS of sts, k4, slip 3 sts purlwise with yarn at WS, k5.

Row 8 Using B, k5, slip 3 sts purlwise with yarn at WS of sts, k4, slip 3 sts purlwise with yarn at WS, k5.

Row 9 Using A, k3, C5B, k4, C5F, k3.

Row 10 Using A, k3, p3, k8, p3, k3.

Row 11 Using B, k3, slip 3 sts purlwise with yarn at WS of sts, k8, slip 3 sts purlwise with yarn at WS, k3.

Row 12 Using B, k3, slip 3 sts purlwise with yarn at WS of sts, k8, slip 3 sts purlwise with yarn at WS, k3.

Row 13 Using A, k2, C4B, k8, C4F, k2.

Row 14 Using A, k2, p3, k10, p3, k2.

Row 15 Using B, k2, slip 3 sts purlwise with yarn at WS of sts, k10, slip 3 sts purlwise with yarn at WS, k2.

Row 16 Using B, k2, slip 3 sts purlwise with yarn at WS of sts, k10, slip 3 sts purlwise with yarn at WS, k2.

Row 17 Using A, knit to end.

Row 18 Using A, k2, p3, k10, p3, k2.

Row 19 As row 15.

Row 20 As row 16.

Row 21 Using A, k2, C4F, k8, C4B, k2.

Row 22 Using A, k3, p3, k8, p3, k3.

Row 23 As row 11.

Row 24 As row 12.

Row 25 Using A, k3, C5F, k4, C5B, k3.

Row 26 Using A, k5, p3, k4, p3, k5.

Row 27 As row 7.

Row 28 As row 8.

Row 29 Using A, k5, C5F, C5B, k5.

Row 30 Using A, k7, p6, k7.

Row 31 As row 3.

Row 32 As row 4.

Repeat these 32 rows.

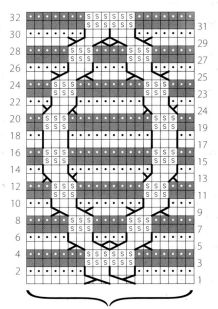

Panel of 20 stitches

KEY

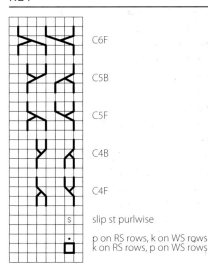

C6F

C5B

C5F

C4B

C4F

s slip st purlwise

· p on RS rows, k on WS rows

□ k on RS rows, p on WS rows

CABLE STITCHES

Diagonal Cable

Abbreviations:

C4B – sl 2 sts on to cable needle at back, k2, then k2 from cable needle.
C4F – sl 2 sts on to cable needle at front, k2, then k2 from cable needle.

Panel of 33 sts.
Row 1 (RS) (P1, k4) 3 times, p3, (k4, p1) 3 times.
Row 2 (K1, p4) 3 times, k3, (p4, k1) 3 times.
Row 3 (P1, C4B) 3 times, p3, (C4F, p1) 3 times.
Row 4 As row 2.
Row 5 P1, k3, (p1, k4) twice, (p1, k1) twice, p1, (k4, p1) twice, k3, p1.
Row 6 K1, p3, (k1, p4) twice, (k1, p1) twice, k1, (p4, k1) twice, p3, k1.
Row 7 P1, k3, (p1, C4B) twice, (p1, k1) twice, p1, (C4F, p1) twice, k3, p1.
Row 8 As row 6.
Row 9 P1, k2, (p1, k4) twice, (p1, k2) twice, (p1, k4) twice, p1, k2, p1.
Row 10 K1, p2, (k1, p4) twice, (k1, p2) twice, (k1, p4) twice, k1, p2, k1.
Row 11 P1, k2, (p1, C4B) twice, (p1, k2) twice, (p1, C4F) twice, p1, k2, p1.
Row 12 As row 10.
Row 13 P1, k1, (p1, k4) twice, (p1, k3) twice, (p1, k4) twice, p1, k1, p1.
Row 14 K1, p1, (k1, p4) twice, (k1, p3) twice, (k1, p4) twice, k1, p1, k1.
Row 15 P1, k1, (p1, C4B) twice, (p1, k3) twice, (p1, C4F) twice, p1, k1, p1.

Row 16 As row 14.
Row 17 P2, (k4, p1) 6 times, p1.
Row 18 K2, (p4, k1) 6 times, k1.
Row 19 P2, (C4B, p1) 3 times, (C4F, p1) 3 times, p1.
Row 20 As row 18.
Repeat these 20 rows.

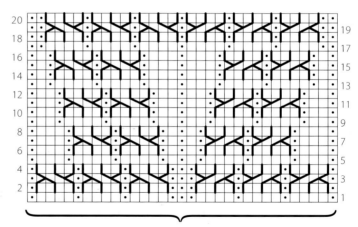

Panel of 33 stitches

KEY

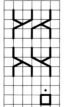

C4B

C4F

p on RS rows, k on WS rows
k on RS rows, p on WS rows

CABLE STITCHES

Aran Diamond and Bobble

Abbreviations:

C5B – sl 3 sts on to cable needle at back, k2, then slip p st from cable needle back to LH needle and p it, then k2 from cable needle.

Cr3R – sl 1 st on to cable needle at back, k2, then p1 from cable needle.

Cr3L – sl 2 sts on to cable needle at front, p1, then k2 from cable needle.

MB – (k1, yo, k1, yo, k1) all into next st, turn and p5, turn and k5, turn and p2tog, p1, p2tog, turn and k3tog.

Panel of 17 sts.

Row 1 (RS) P6, C5B, p6.
Row 2 K6, p2, k1, p2, k6.
Row 3 P5, Cr3R, k1, Cr3L, p5.
Row 4 K5, p2, k1, p1, k1, p2, k5.
Row 5 P4, Cr3R, k1, p1, k1, Cr3L, p4.
Row 6 K4, p2, (k1, p1) twice, k1, p2, k4.
Row 7 P3, Cr3R, (k1, p1) twice, k1, Cr3L, p3.
Row 8 K3, p2, (k1, p1) 3 times, k1, p2, k3.
Row 9 P2, Cr3R, (k1, p1) 3 times, k1, Cr3L, p2.
Row 10 K2, p2, (k1, p1) 4 times, k1, p2, k2.
Row 11 P2, Cr3L, (p1, k1) 3 times, p1, Cr3R, p2.
Row 12 As row 8.
Row 13 P3, Cr3L, (p1, k1) twice, p1, Cr3R, p3.
Row 14 As row 6.
Row 15 P4, Cr3L, p1, k1, p1, Cr3R, p4.
Row 16 As row 4.
Row 17 P5, Cr3L, p1, Cr3R, p5.

Row 18 As row 2.
Row 19 As row 1.
Row 20 As row 2.
Row 21 P5, Cr3R, p1, Cr3L, p5.
Row 22 K5, p2, k3, p2, k5.
Row 23 P4, Cr3R, p3, Cr3L, p4.
Row 24 K4, p2, k5, p2, k4.
Row 25 P4, k2, p2, MB, p2, k2, p4.
Row 26 As row 24.
Row 27 P4, Cr3L, p3, Cr3R, p4.
Row 28 As row 22.
Row 29 P5, Cr3L, p1, Cr3R, p5.
Row 30 As row 2.
Repeat these 30 rows.

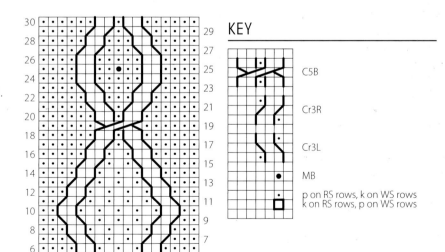

Panel of 17 stitches

KEY

C5B

Cr3R

Cr3L

● MB

· p on RS rows, k on WS rows
□ k on RS rows, p on WS rows

CABLE FABRICS

Woven Cables

Abbreviations:

C4F – sl 2 sts on to cable needle at front, k2, then k2 from cable needle.
C4B – sl 2 sts on to cable needle at back, k2, then k2 from cable needle.

Multiple of 8 sts plus 2.
Row 1 (RS) Knit.
Row 2 and every foll WS row Purl.
Row 3 K1, * C4B; rep from * to last st, k1.
Row 5 Knit.
Row 7 K3, * C4F; rep from * to last 3 sts, k3.
Row 8 Purl.
Repeat these 8 rows.

Honeycomb Fabric

Abbreviations:

C4F – sl 2 sts on to cable needle at front, k2, then k2 from cable needle.
C4B – sl 2 sts on to cable needle at back, k2, then k2 from cable needle.

Multiple of 12 sts plus 10.
Row 1 (RS) K3, p2, * p2, k8, p2; rep from * to last 5 sts, p2, k3.
Row 2 and every foll WS row Purl.
Row 3 K1, C4B, * C4F, k4, C4B; rep from * to last 5 sts, C4F, k1.
Row 5 K5, * k4, p4, k4; rep from * to last 5 sts, k5.
Row 7 K5, * k2, C4B, C4F, k2; rep from * to last 5 sts, k5.
Row 8 Purl.
Repeat these 8 rows.

Cable Rings

Abbreviations:

C4F – sl 2 sts on to cable needle at front, k2, then k2 from cable needle.
C4B – sl 2 sts on to cable needle at back, k2, then k2 from cable needle.

Multiple of 16 sts plus 2.
Row 1 (RS) Knit.
Row 2 and every foll WS row Purl.
Row 3 K1, * C4B, C4F, k8; rep from * to last st, k1.
Row 5 Knit.
Row 7 K1, * C4F, C4B, k8; rep from * to last st, k1.
Row 9 Knit.
Row 11 K1, * k8, C4B, C4F; rep from * to last st, k1.
Row 13 Knit.
Row 15 K1, * k8, C4F, C4B; rep from * to last st, k1.
Row 16 Purl.
Repeat these 16 rows.

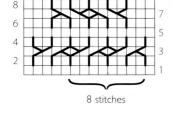

8 stitches

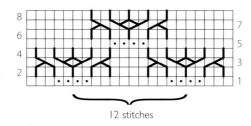

12 stitches

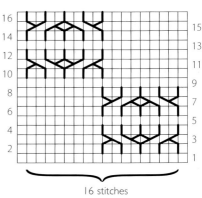

16 stitches

KEY

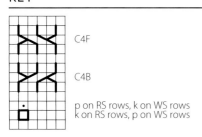

C4F

C4B

p on RS rows, k on WS rows
k on RS rows, p on WS rows

CABLE FABRICS

Open Cables

Abbreviation:
C5B – sl 3 sts on to cable needle at back, k2, then k3 from cable needle.

Multiple of 24 sts plus 1.

Row 1 (RS) K3, ssk, yo, k2, p3, * C5B, p3, k2, yo, k2tog, k5, ssk, yo, k2, p3; rep from * to last 15 sts, C5B, p3, k2, yo, k2tog, k3.

Row 2 and every foll WS row Purl.

Row 3 K3, ssk, yo, k2, p3, * k5, p3, k2, yo, k2tog, k5, ssk, yo, k2, p3; rep from * to last 15 sts, k5, p3, k2, yo, k2tog, k3.

Row 5 K4, yo, k2tog, k1, p3, * C5B, p3, k1, ssk, yo, k7, yo, k2tog, k1, p3; rep from * to last 15 sts, C5B, p3, k1, ssk, yo, k4.

Row 7 K2, ssk, yo, k2tog, k1, p3, k1, * (k1, yo) twice, k2, p3, k1, ssk, yo, k2tog, k3, ssk, yo, k2tog, k1, p3, k1; rep from * to last 14 sts, (k1, yo) twice, k2, p3, k1, ssk, yo, k2tog, k2.

Row 9 K1, ssk, yo, k2tog, k1, p3, k2, * yo, k3, yo, k2, p3, (k1, ssk, yo, k2tog) twice, k1, p3, k2; rep from * to last 14 sts, yo, k3, yo, k2, p3, k1, ssk, yo, k2tog, k1.

Row 11 Ssk, yo, k2tog, k1, p3, k2, yo, * k5, yo, k2, p3, k1, ssk, yo, sk2po, yo, k2tog, k1, p3, k2, yo; rep from * to last 15 sts, k5, yo, k2, p3, k1, ssk, yo, k2tog.

Row 13 K2tog, k2, p3, k2, yo, k1, * k6, yo, k2, p3, k2, sl2tog-k1-psso, k2, p3, k2, yo, k1; rep from * to last 15 sts, k6, yo, k2, p3, k2, ssk.

Row 15 K3, p3, k2, yo, k2tog, * k5, ssk, yo, k2, p3, C5B, p3, k2, yo, k2tog; rep from * to last 15 sts, k5, ssk, yo, k2, p3, k3.

Row 17 K3, p3, k2, yo, k2tog, * k5, ssk, yo, k2, p3, k5, p3, k2, yo, k2tog; rep from * to last 15 sts, k5, ssk, yo, k2, p3, k3.

Row 19 K3, p3, k1, ssk, yo, k1, * k6, yo, k2tog, k1, p3, C5B, p3, k1, ssk, yo, k1; rep from * to last 15 sts, k6, yo, k2tog, k1, p3, k3.

Row 21 K1, yo, k2, p3, k1, ssk, yo, * k2tog, k3, ssk, yo, k2tog, k1, p3, k2, yo, k1, yo, k2, p3, k1, ssk, yo; rep from * to last 15 sts, k2tog, k3, ssk, yo, k2tog, k1, p3, k2, yo, k1.

Row 23 K2, yo, k2, p3, k1, ssk, * yo, k2tog, k1, ssk, yo, k2tog, k1, p3, k2, yo, k3, yo, k2,

p3, k1, ssk; rep from * to last 15 sts, yo, k2tog, k1, ssk, yo, k2tog, k1, p3, k2, yo, k2.

Row 25 K3, yo, k2, p3, k1, * ssk, yo, sk2po, yo, k2tog, k1, p3, k2, yo, k5, yo, k2, p3, k1; rep from * to last 15 sts, ssk, yo, sk2po, yo, k2tog, k1, p3, k2, yo, k3.

Row 27 K4, yo, k2, p3, * k2, sl2tog-k1-psso, k2, p3, k2, yo, k7, yo, k2, p3; rep from * to last 15 sts, k2, sl2tog-k1-psso, k2, p3, k2, yo, k4.

Row 28 Purl.
Repeat these 28 rows.

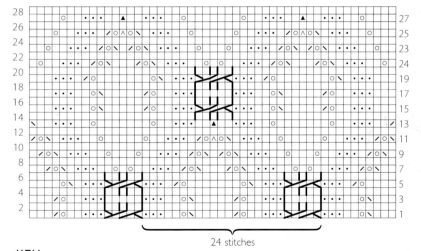

24 stitches

KEY

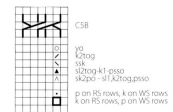

C5B

o	yo
/	k2tog
\	ssk
▲	sl2tog-k1-psso
ʌ	sk2po - sl1,k2tog,psso
•	p on RS rows, k on WS rows
□	k on RS rows, p on WS rows

CABLE FABRICS

Trellis with Moss Stitch

Abbreviations:

C5F – sl 2 sts on to cable needle at front, k3, then k2 from cable needle.

C3B – sl 1 st on to cable needle at back, k2, then k1 from cable needle.

C3F – sl 2 sts on to cable needle at front, k1, then k2 from cable needle.

Cr3R – sl 1 st on to cable needle at back, k2, then p1 from cable needle.

Cr3L – sl 2 sts on to cable needle at front, p1, then k2 from cable needle.

Multiple of 12 sts plus 1.

Row 1 (WS) * K4, p2, k1, p2, k3; rep from * to last st, k1.

Row 2 P1, * p3, C5F, p4; rep from * to end.

Row 3 * K4, p5, k3; rep from * to last st, k1.

Row 4 P1, * p2, C3B, p1, C3F, p3; rep from * to end.

Row 5 * K3, p3, k1, p3, k2; rep from * to last st, k1.

Row 6 P1, * p1, C3B, p1, k1, p1, C3F, p2; rep from * to end.

Row 7 * K2, p3, k1, p1, k1, p3, k1; rep from * to last st, k1.

Row 8 P1, * C3B, (p1, k1) twice, p1, C3F, p1; rep from * to end.

Row 9 * K1, p3, (k1, p1) twice, k1, p3; rep from * to last st, k1.

Row 10 P1, k2, * (p1, k1) 3 times, p1, C5F; rep from * to last 10 sts, (p1, k1) 3 times, p1, k2, p1.

Row 11 * K1, p2, (k1, p1) 3 times, k1, p2; rep from * to last st, k1.

Row 12 P1, * Cr3L, (p1, k1) twice, p1, Cr3R, p1; rep from * to end.

Row 13 * K2, p2, (k1, p1) twice, k1, p2, k1; rep from * to last st, k1.

Row 14 P1, * p1, Cr3L, p1, k1, p1, Cr3R, p2; rep from * to end.

Row 15 * K3, p2, k1, p1, k1, p2, k2; rep from * to last st, k1.

Row 16 P1, * p2, Cr3L, p1, Cr3R, p3; rep from * to end.

Repeat these 16 rows.

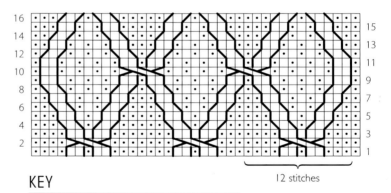

12 stitches

KEY

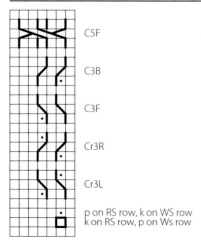

C5F

C3B

C3F

Cr3R

Cr3L

p on RS row, k on WS row
k on RS row, p on Ws row

TWIST STITCHES

Twist Stitch Chevron

Panel of 16 sts.

Foundation Row (WS) K7, p2, k7.

Row 1 (RS) P7, RT, p7.

Row 2 K7, p2, k7.

Row 3 P6, RT, LT, p6.

Row 4 K6, p4, k6.

Row 5 P5, RT, k2, LT, p5.

Row 6 K5, p1, k1, p2, k1, p1, k5.

Row 7 P4, RT, k4, LT, p4.

Row 8 K4, p1, k2, p2, k2, p1, k4.

Row 9 P3, RT, k6, LT, p3.

Row 10 K3, p1, k3, p2, k3, p1, k3.

Row 11 P2, RT, k8, LT, p2.

Row 12 K2, p1, k4, p2, k4, p1, k2.

Row 13 P1, RT, k3, RT, LT, k3, LT, p1.

Row 14 K1, p1, k4, p4, k4, p1, k1.

Row 15 P1, k4, RT, k2, LT, k4, p1.

Row 16 K1, p1, k3, p1, k1, p2, k1, p1, k3, p1, k1.

Row 17 P1, k3, RT, p1, RT, p1, LT, k3, p1.

Row 18 K1, (p1, k2) twice, p2, (k2, p1) twice, k1.

Row 19 P1, k2, RT, p2, k2, p2, LT, k2, p1.

Row 20 (K1, p1) twice, k3, p2, k3, (p1, k1) twice.

Row 21 P1, k1, RT, p3, RT, p3, LT, k1, p1.

Row 22 K1, (p2, k4) twice, p2, k1.

Row 23 P1, RT, p4, k2, p4, LT, p1.

Row 24 K7, p2, k7.

Repeat these 24 rows.

Braid

Panel of 10 sts.

Foundation Row (WS) K3, p5, k2.

Row 1 (RS) P2, k3, RT, p3.

Row 2 K3, p5, k2.

Row 3 P2, LT, RT, LT, p2.

Row 4 K2, p5, k3.

Row 5 P3, LT, k3, p2.

Row 6 As row 4.

Row 7 P2, RT, LT, RT, p2.

Row 8 As row 2.

Repeat these 8 rows.

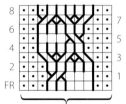

Panel of 10 stitches

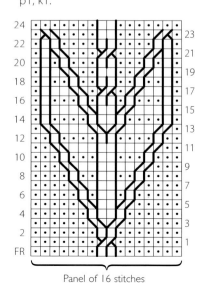

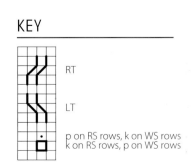

Panel of 16 stitches

KEY

RT

LT

p on RS rows, k on WS rows
k on RS rows, p on WS rows

Abbreviations:

RT – (right twist) take RH needle in front of first st on LH needle and knit 2nd st, then knit first st, slip both sts off needle.

LT – (left twist) take RH needle behind first st on LH needle and knit 2nd st, then knit first st, slip both sts off needle.

TWIST STITCHES

Twist Stitch Hearts

Panel of 12 sts.
Row 1 (RS) P12.
Row 2 K5, p2, k5.
Row 3 P4, RT, LT, p4.
Row 4 K4, p4, k4.
Row 5 P3, RT, k2, LT, p3.
Row 6 K3, p6, k3.
Row 7 P2, RT, k4, LT, p2.
Row 8 K2, p8, k2.
Row 9 P1, RT, k6, LT, p1.
Row 10 K1, p10, k1.
Row 11 P1, k3, RT, LT, k3, p1.
Row 12 K1, p4, k2, p4, k1.
Row 13 P1, LT, RT, p2, LT, RT, p1.
Row 14 K2, p2, k4, p2, k2.
Row 15 P2, RT, p4, LT, p2.
Row 16 K12.
Repeat these 16 rows.

Twist Stitch Cables

Multiple of 12 sts plus 2.
Foundation Row (WS) * K3, p2, k3, p4; rep from * to last 2 sts, k2.
Row 1 (RS) P2, * k4, p3, RT, p3; rep from * to end.
Row 2 * K3, p2, k3, p4; rep from * to last 2 sts, k2.
Row 3 P2, * LT, RT, p2, RT, LT, p2; rep from * to end.
Row 4 K2, * p4, k3, p2, k3; rep from * to end.
Row 5 * P3, RT, p3, k4; rep from * to last 2 sts, p2.
Row 6 As row 4.
Row 7 P2, * RT, LT, p2, LT, RT, p2; rep from * to end.
Row 8 * K3, p2, k3, p4; rep from * to last 2 sts, k2.
Repeat these 8 rows.

Abbreviations:
RT – (right twist) take RH needle in front of first st on LH needle and knit 2nd st, then knit first st, slip both sts off needle.
LT – (left twist) take RH needle behind first st on LH needle and knit 2nd st, then knit first st, slip both sts off needle.

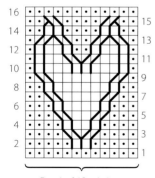

Panel of 12 stitches

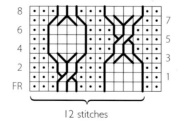

12 stitches

KEY

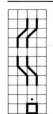

RT

LT

p on RS rows, k on WS rows
k on RS rows, p on WS rows

TWIST STITCHES

Lattice

Multiple of 8 sts plus 2.

Row 1 (RS) K1, * LT, k4, RT; rep from * to last st, k1.

Row 2 and every foll WS row Purl.

Row 3 K1, * k1, LT, k2, RT, k1; rep from * to last st, k1.

Row 5 K1, * k2, LT, RT, k2; rep from * to last st, k1.

Row 7 K1, * k3, RT, k3; rep from * to last st, k1.

Row 9 K1, * k2, RT, LT, k2; rep from * to last st, k1.

Row 11 K1, * k1, RT, k2, LT, k1; rep from * to last st, k1.

Row 13 K1, * RT, k4, LT; rep from * to last st, k1.

Row 15 K2, * k6, LT; rep from * to last 8 sts, k8.

Row 16 Purl.

Repeat these 16 rows.

Tent Stitch

Multiple of 14 sts plus 2.

Foundation Row (WS) K1, * p3, k8, p3; rep from * to last st, k1.

Row 1 (RS) P1, * LT, LT, p6, RT, RT; rep from * to last st, p1.

Row 2 K1, * k1, p3, k6, p3, k1; rep from * to last st, k1.

Row 3 P1, * p1, LT, LT, p4, RT, RT, p1; rep from * to last st, p1.

Row 4 K1, * k2, p3, k4, p3, k2; rep from * to last st, k1.

Row 5 P1, * p2, LT, LT, p2, RT, RT, p2; rep from * to last st, p1.

Row 6 K1, * k3, p3, k2, p3, k3; rep from * to last st, k1.

Row 7 P1, * p3, LT, LT, RT, RT, p3; rep from * to last st, p1.

Row 8 K1, * k4, p6, k4; rep from * to last st, k1.

Row 9 P1, * p4, LT, k2, RT, p4; rep from * to last st, p1.

Row 10 K1, * k5, p4, k5; rep from * to last st, k1.

Row 11 P1, * p5, LT, RT, p5; rep from * to last st, p1.

Row 12 K1, * p3, k3, p2, k3, p3; rep from * to last st, k1.

Repeat these 12 rows.

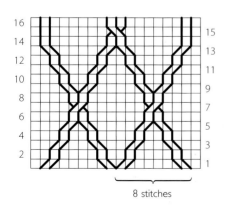

8 stitches

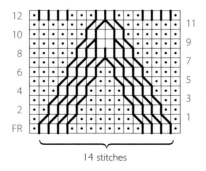

14 stitches

EMBOSSED FABRICS

Bell Motif

Multiple of 4 sts (stitch count varies).
Foundation Row (WS) Purl.
Row 1 (RS) P4, * turn work and cast on 8 sts, turn work back, p4; rep from * to end. 12 sts.
Row 2 * K4, p8; rep from * to last 4 sts, k4.
Row 3 P4, * k8, p4; rep from * to end.
Row 4 As row 2.
Row 5 P4, * ssk, k4, k2tog, p4; rep from * to end. 10 sts.
Row 6 * K4, p6; rep from * to last 4 sts, k4.
Row 7 P4, * ssk, k2, k2tog, p4; rep from * to end. 8 sts.
Row 8 * K4, p4; rep from * to last 4 sts, k4.
Row 9 P4, * ssk, k2tog, p4; rep from * to end. 6 sts.
Row 10 * K4, p2; rep from * to last 4 sts, k4.
Row 11 P4, * k2tog, p4; rep from * to end. 5 sts.
Row 12 * K4, p1; rep from * to last 4 sts, k4.
Row 13 P4, * p2tog, p3; rep from * to end. 4 sts.
Row 14 K to end.
Repeat these 14 rows.

Bobble Lattice

Abbreviation:
MB – make a bobble by (k1, p1, k1, p1, k1, p1) all into next st, then lift 2nd, 3rd, 4th, 5th and 6th sts over first st.

Multiple of 10 sts plus 3.
Row 1 (RS) P1, * p5, MB, p4; rep from * to last 2 sts, p2.
Row 2 and every foll WS row K to end.
Row 3 P1, * p4, MB, p1, MB, p3; rep from * to last 2 sts, p2.
Row 5 P1, * p3, MB, p3, MB, p2; rep from * to last 2 sts, p2.
Row 7 P1, * p2, MB, p5, MB, p1; rep from * to last 2 sts, p2.
Row 9 P1, * p1, MB, p7, MB; rep from * to last 2 sts, p2.
Row 11 P1, * MB, p9; rep from * to last 2 sts, MB, p1.
Row 13 As row 9.
Row 15 As row 7.
Row 17 As row 5.
Row 19 As row 3.
Row 20 K to end.
Repeat these 20 rows.

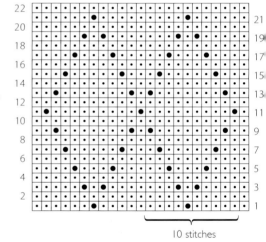

10 stitches

KEY

| | MB |
| | p on RS rows, k on WS rows
k on RS rows, p on WS rows |

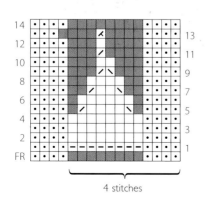

4 stitches

KEY

–	cast on st
/	k2tog
⋏	p2tog
	ssk
	p on RS rows, k on WS rows k on RS rows, p on WS rows no stitch

EMBOSSED FABRICS

Bud Stitch

Abbreviation:
sl3tog-k2tog-p3sso – slip 3 sts together as though to k3tog, then knit the next 2 sts together, then pass the 3 slipped sts over together.

Multiple of 10 sts plus 2 (stitch count varies).
Foundation Row (WS) Purl.
Row 1 (RS) * K8, (k1, yo, k1, yo, k1) all into next st, k1; rep from * to last 2 sts, k2. 16 sts.
Row 2 P2, * p1, purl the 5 new sts wrapping yarn twice around the needle for each st, p8; rep from * to end. 16 sts.
Row 3 * K8, slip 5 new sts with yarn at WS of work dropping extra wraps, k1; rep from * to last 2 sts, k2.
Row 4 P2, * p1, slip 5 new sts with yarn at WS of work, p8; rep from * to end.
Row 5 * K8, sl3tog-k2tog-p3sso, k1; rep from * to last 2 sts, k2. 12sts.
Row 6 Purl.
Row 7 * K3, (k1, yo, k1, yo, k1) all into next st, k6; rep from * to last 2 sts, k2. 16 sts.
Row 8 P2, * p6, purl the 5 new sts wrapping yarn twice around the needle for each st, p3; rep from * to end.
Row 9 * K3, slip 5 new sts with yarn at WS of work dropping extra wraps, k6; rep from * to last 2 sts, k2.
Row 10 P2, * p6, slip 5 new sts with yarn at WS of work, p3; rep from * to end.
Row 11 * K3, sl3tog-k2tog-p3sso, k6; rep from * to last 2 sts, k2. 12 sts.
Row 12 Purl.
Repeat these 12 rows.

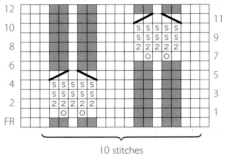

10 stitches

KEY

o	yo
⌃	sl3tog-k2tog-p3sso slip stitch
s / 2	yarn twice round needle
☐	k on RS rows, p on WS rows
	no stitch

KEY

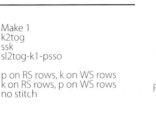

M	Make 1
∕	k2tog
＼	ssk
▲	sl2tog-k1-psso
•	p on RS rows, k on WS rows
☐	k on RS rows, p on WS rows
	no stitch

Puff Stitch

Abbreviation:
M1 – make one by picking up the strand between sts and knitting into the back of it.

Multiple of 10 sts plus 2.
Foundation Row (WS) K2, * p5, k2, p1, k2; rep from * to end.
Row 1 (RS) * P2, M1, k1, M1, p2, ssk, k1, k2tog; rep from * to last 2 sts, p2.
Row 2 K2, * p3, k2; rep from * to end.
Row 3 * P2, M1, k3, M1, p2, sl2tog-k1-psso; rep from * to last 2 sts, p2.
Row 4 K2, * p1, k2, p5, k2; rep from * to end.
Row 5 * P2, ssk, k1, k2tog, p2, M1, k1, M1; rep from * to last 2 sts, p2.
Row 6 As row 2.
Row 7 * P2, sl2tog-k1-psso, p2, M1, k3, M1; rep from * to last 2 sts, p2.
Row 8 K2, * p5, k2, p1, k2; rep from * to end.
Repeat these 8 rows.

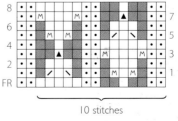

10 stitches

EMBOSSED FABRICS

Bobble Heart

Abbreviation:

MB – make a bobble by (k1, p1, k1, p1, k1, p1) all into next st, then lift 2nd, 3rd, 4th, 5th and 6th sts over first st.

Panel of 13 sts.
Row 1 (RS) P6, MB, p6.
Row 2 and every foll WS row K13.
Row 3 P5, MB, p1, MB, p5.
Row 5 P4, MB, p3, MB, p4.
Row 7 P3, MB, p5, MB, p3.
Row 9 P2, MB, p7, MB, p2.
Row 11 P1, MB, p4, MB, p4, MB, p1.
Row 13 P1, MB, p3, MB, p1, MB, p3, MB, p1.
Row 15 P2, MB, p1, MB, p3, MB, p1, MB, p2.
Row 16 K13.

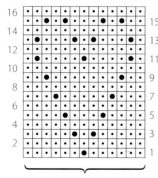

Panel of 13 stitches

Bobble Flower

Abbreviation:

MB – make a bobble by (k1, p1, k1, p1, k1, p1) all into next st, then lift 2nd, 3rd, 4th, 5th and 6th sts over first st.

Panel of 21 sts.
Row 1 (RS) (P5, MB, p1, MB) twice, p5.
Row 2 and every foll WS row K21.
Row 3 P3, MB, p5, MB, p1, MB, p5, MB, p3.
Row 5 P3, (MB, p6) twice, MB, p3.
Row 7 As row 5.
Row 9 P5, MB, p9, MB, p5.
Row 11 P3, (MB, p1) twice, MB, p5, (MB, p1) twice, MB, p3.
Row 13 P1, MB, p17, MB, p1.
Row 15 As row 13.
Row 17 P1, (MB, p5) 3 times, MB, p1.
Row 19 P2, (MB, p1) twice, MB, p7, (MB, p1) twice, MB, p2.
Row 21 P7, MB, p5, MB, p7.
Row 23 As row 21.
Row 25 P8, (MB, p1) twice, MB, p8.
Row 26 K21.

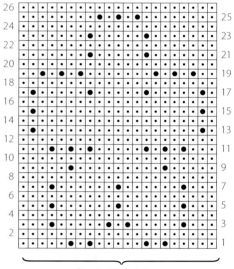

Panel of 21 stitches

KEY

●	MB
·	p on RS rows, k on WS rows
☐	k on RS rows, p on WS rows

EMBOSSED FABRICS

Embossed Blocks

Multiple of 18 sts plus 1.

Foundation Row (WS) P1, * k3, p11, k3, p1; rep from * to end.

Row 1 * K1, M1, p3, ssk, k7, k2tog, p3, M1; rep from * to last st, k1.

Row 2 P1, * p1, k3, p9, k3, p2; rep from * to end.

Row 3 * K2, M1, p3, ssk, k5, k2tog, p3, M1, k1; rep from * to last st, k1.

Row 4 P1, * p2, k3, p7, k3, p3; rep from * to end.

Row 5 * K3, M1, p3, ssk, k3, k2tog, p3, M1, k2; rep from * to last st, k1.

Row 6 P1, * p3, k3, p5, k3, p4; rep from * to end.

Row 7 * K4, M1, p3, ssk, k1, k2tog, p3, M1, k3; rep from * to last st, k1.

Row 8 P1, * p4, k3, p3, k3, p5; rep from * to end.

Row 9 * K5, M1, p3, sk2po, p3, M1, k4; rep from * to last st, k1.

Row 10 P1, * p5, k3, p1, k3, p6; rep from * to end.

Row 11 * K4, k2tog, p3, M1, k1, M1, p3, ssk, k3; rep from * to last st, k1.

Row 12 P1, * P4, k3, p3, k3, p5; rep from * to end.

Row 13 * K3, k2tog, p3, M1, k3, M1, p3, ssk, k2; rep from * to last st, k1.

Row 14 P1, * p3, k3, p5, k3, p4; rep from * to end.

Row 15 * K2, k2tog, p3, M1, k5, M1, p3, ssk, k1; rep from * to last st, k1.

Row 16 P1, * p2, k3, p7, k3, p3; rep from * to end.

Row 17 * K1, k2tog, p3, M1, k7, M1, p3, ssk; rep from * to last st, k1.

Row 18 P1, * p1, k3, p9, k3, p2; rep from * to end.

Row 19 K2tog, * p3, M1, k9, M1, p3, sk2po; rep from * to last 17 sts, p3, M1, k9, M1, p3, ssk.

Row 20 P1, * k3, p11, k3, p1; rep from * to end.

Repeat these 20 rows.

KEY

M	M1
∕	k2tog
╲	ssk
∧	sk2po
•	p on RS rows, k on WS rows
☐	K on RS rows, p on WS rows

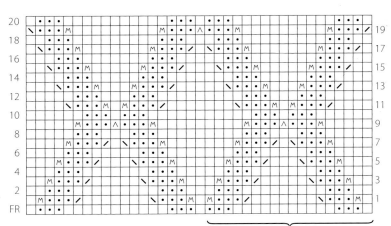

18 stitches

EMBOSSED FABRICS

Leaf Pattern

Multiple of 8 sts plus 7 (stitch count varies).

Row 1 (RS) * P7, k1; rep from * to last 7 sts, p7.
Row 2 K7, * p1, k7; rep from * to end.
Row 3 * P7, M1, k1, M1; rep from * to last 7 sts, p7. 10 sts.
Row 4 K7, * p3, k7; rep from * to end.
Row 5 * P7, k1, yo, k1, yo, k1; rep from * to last 7 sts, p7. 12 sts.
Row 6 K7, * p5, k7; rep from * to end.
Row 7 * P7, k2, yo, k1, yo, k2; rep from * to last 7 sts, p7. 14 sts.
Row 8 K7, * p7, k7; rep from * to end.
Row 9 * P7, k2, sl2tog-k1-psso, k2; rep from * to last 7 sts, p7. 12 sts.
Row 10 As row 6.

Row 11 * P7, k1, sl2tog-k1-psso, k1; rep from * to last 7 sts, p7. 10 sts.
Row 12 As row 4.
Row 13 * P7, sl2tog-k1-psso; rep from * to last 7 sts, p7. 8 sts.
Row 14 As row 2.
Row 15 * P3, k1, p4; rep from * to last 7 sts, p3, k1, p3.
Row 16 K3, p1, k3, * k4, p1, k3; rep from * to end.
Row 17 * P3, M1, k1, M1, p4; rep from * to last 7 sts, p3, M1, k1, M1, p3. 10 sts.
Row 18 K3, p3, k3, * k4, p3, k3; rep from * to end.
Row 19 * P3, k1, yo, k1, yo, k1, p4; rep from * to last 9 sts, p3, k1, yo, k1, yo, k1, p3. 12 sts.

Row 20 K3, p5, k3, * k4, p5, k3; rep from * to end.
Row 21 * P3, k2, yo, k1, yo, k2, p4; rep from * to last 11 sts, p3, k2, yo, k1, yo, k2, p3. 14 sts.
Row 22 K3, p7, k3, * k4, p7, k3; rep from * to end.
Row 23 * P3, k2, sl2tog-k1-psso, k2, p4; rep from * to last 13 sts, p3, k2, sl2tog-k1-psso, k2, p3. 12 sts.
Row 24 As row 20.
Row 25 * P3, k1, sl2tog-k1-psso, k1, p4; rep from * to last 11 sts, p3, k1, sl2tog-k1-psso, k1, p3. 10 sts.
Row 26 As row 18.
Row 27 * P3, sl2tog-k1-psso, p4; rep from * to last 9 sts, p3, sl2tog-k1-psso, p3. 8 sts.
Row 28 As row 16.
Repeat these 28 rows.

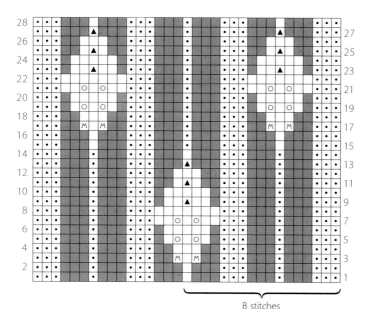

8 stitches

KEY

O	yo
M	Make1
▲	sl2tog-k1-psso
	p on RS rows, k on WS rows
☐	k on RS rows, p on WS rows
	no stitch

LACE STITCHES

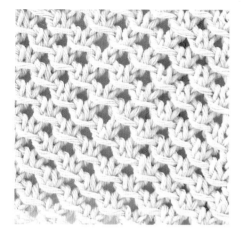

Lace Mesh

Multiple of 3 sts (cast on a minimum of 6 sts).
Row 1 K2, * yo, sl 1, k2, psso the 2 k sts; rep from * to last st, k1.
Row 2 Purl.
Row 3 K1, * sl 1, k2, psso the 2 k sts, yo; rep from * to last 2 sts, k2.
Row 4 Purl.
Repeat these 4 rows.

Zig Zag Lace

Multiple of 10 sts.
Row 1 (RS) * K2, p3, k2tog, yo, k3; rep from * to end.
Row 2 and every WS row Purl.
Row 3 * K1, p3, k2tog, yo, k4; rep from * to end.
Row 5 * P3, k2tog, yo, k5; rep from * to end.
Row 7 * K3, yo, ssk, p3, k2; rep from * to end.
Row 9 * K4, yo, ssk, p3, k1; rep from * to end.
Row 11 * K5, yo, ssk, p3; rep from * to end.
Row 12 Purl.
Repeat these 12 rows.

Vine Lace Zig Zag

Multiple of 10 sts plus 1.
Row 1 (RS) K1, * k2tog, k4, yo, k1, yo, ssk, k1; rep from * to end.
Row 2 and every foll WS row Purl.
Row 3 K1, * k2tog, k3, (yo, k1) twice, ssk, k1; rep from * to end.
Row 5 K1, * k2tog, k2, yo, k1, yo, k2, ssk, k1; rep from * to end.
Row 7 K1, * k2tog, (k1, yo) twice, k3, ssk, k1; rep from * to end.
Row 9 K1, * k2tog, yo, k1, yo, k4, ssk, k1; rep from * to end.
Row 11 K1, * k2tog, (k1, yo) twice, k3, ssk, k1; rep from * to end.
Row 13 K1, * k2tog, k2, yo, k1, yo, k2, ssk, k1; rep from * to end.
Row 15 K1, * k2tog, k3, (yo, k1) twice, ssk, k1; rep from * to end.
Row 16 Purl.
Repeat these 16 rows.

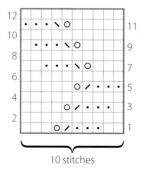

10 stitches

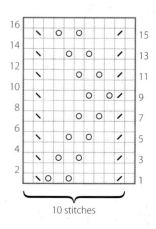

10 stitches

KEY

O	yo
╱	k2tog
╲	ssk
•	p on RS rows, k on WS rows
☐	k on RS rows, p on WS rows

LACE STITCHES

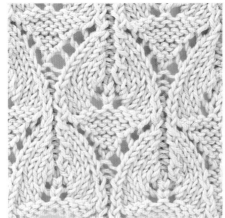

Crest of the Wave

Multiple of 12 sts plus 1.
Rows 1 to 4 Knit.
Rows 5, 7, 9 and 11 K1, * (k2tog) twice, (yo, k1) 3 times, yo, (ssk) twice, k1; rep from * to end.
Rows 6, 8, 10 and 12 Purl.
Repeat these 12 rows.

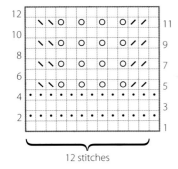

12 stitches

Gothic Window

Multiple of 12 sts plus 1.
Row 1 (RS) P1, * ssk, k3, yo, k1, yo, k3, k2tog, p1; rep from * to end.
Row 2 * K1, p11; rep from * to last st, k1.
Rows 3 to 6 Rep rows 1 and 2 twice more.
Row 7 P1, * yo, k3, ssk, p1, k2tog, k3, yo, p1; rep from * to end.
Row 8 * K1, p5; rep from * to last st, k1.
Row 9 P1, * p1, yo, k2, ssk, p1, k2tog, k2, yo, p2; rep from * to end.
Row 10 * K2, (p4, k1) twice; rep from * to last st, k1.
Row 11 P1; * p2, yo, k1, ssk, p1, k2tog, k1, yo, p3; rep from * to end.
Row 12 * K3, p3, k1, p3, k2; rep from * to last st, k1.
Row 13 P1, * p3, yo, ssk, p1, k2tog, yo, p4; rep from * to end.
Row 14 * K4, p2, k1, p2, k3; rep from * to last st, k1.
Row 15 K1, * yo, k3, k2tog, p1, ssk, k3, yo, k1; rep from * to end.
Row 16 * P6, k1, p5; rep from * to last st, p1.
Rows 17 to 20 Repeat rows 15 and 16 twice more.
Row 21 P1, * k2tog, k3, yo, p1, yo, k3, ssk, p1; rep from * to end.
Row 22 As row 8.
Row 23 P1, * k2tog, k2, yo, p3, yo, k2, ssk, p1; rep from * to end.

Row 24 * K1, p4, k3, p4; rep from * to last st, k1.
Row 25 P1, * k2tog, k1, yo, p5, yo, k1, ssk, p1; rep from * to end.
Row 26 * K1, p3, k5, p3; rep from * to last st, k1.
Row 27 P1, * k2tog, yo, p7, yo, ssk, p1; rep from * to end.
Row 28 * K1, p2, k7, p2; rep from * to last st, k1.
Repeat these 28 rows.

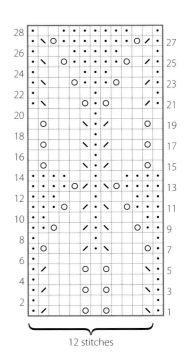

12 stitches

KEY

O	yo
/	k2tog
\	ssk
•	p on RS rows, k on WS rows
□	k on RS rows, p on WS rows

LACE STITCHES

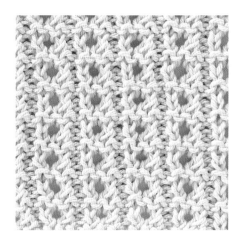

Quatrefoil Eyelets

Multiple of 8 sts plus 7.
Row 1 (RS) K2, * k1, yo, ssk, k5; rep from * to last 5 sts, k1, yo, ssk, k2.
Row 2 and every foll WS row Purl.
Row 3 K1, k2tog, * yo, k1, yo, ssk, k3, k2tog; rep from * to last 5 sts, yo, k1, yo, ssk, k1.
Row 5 As row 1.
Row 7 Knit.
Row 9 K2, * k5, yo, ssk, k1; rep from * to last 5 sts, k5.
Row 11 K2, * k3, k2tog, yo, k1, yo, ssk; rep from * to last 5 sts, k5.
Row 13 As row 9.
Row 15 Knit.
Row 16 Purl.
Repeat these 16 rows.

Quatrefoil Eyelets in Diamonds

Multiple of 12 sts plus 3.
Row 1 (RS) K1, * k1, yo, ssk, k3, p1, k3, k2tog, yo; rep from * to last 2 sts, k2.
Row 2 P2, * p4, k1, p1, k1, p5; rep from * to last st, p1.
Row 3 K1, * yo, ssk, k2, p1, k3 (twice); rep from * to last 2 sts, yo, ssk.
Row 4 P2, * p2, k1, p5, k1, p3; rep from * to last st, p1.
Row 5 K1, * k2, p1, k2, k2tog, yo, k3, p1, k1; rep from * to last 2 sts, k2.
Row 6 P2, * k1, p9, k1, p1; rep from * to last st, p1.
Row 7 K1, * p1, k3, k2tog, yo, k1, yo, ssk, k3; rep from * to last 2 sts, p1, k1.
Row 8 As row 6.
Row 9 K1, * k2, p1, k3, yo, ssk, k2, p1, k1; rep from * to last 2 sts, k2.
Row 10 As row 4.
Row 11 K2tog, * yo, (k3, p1) twice, k2, k2tog; rep from * to last st, yo, k1.
Row 12 As row 2.
Repeat these 12 rows.

Lace Rib

Multiple of 4 sts plus 1.
Row 1 (RS) * P1, k3; rep from * to last st, p1.
Row 2 K1, * p1, yo, p2tog, k1; rep from * to end.
Row 3 As row 1.
Row 4 Knit.
Repeat these 4 rows.

4 stitches

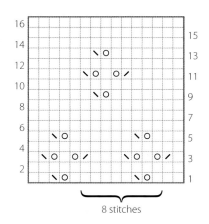

8 stitches

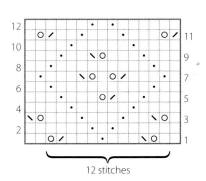

12 stitches

KEY

O	yo
╱	k2tog
╲	ssk
⅄	p2tog
•	p on RS rows, k on WS rows
☐	k on RS rows, p on WS rows

LACE STITCHES

Ridged Feather Stitch

Multiple of 11 sts.
Row 1 (RS) Knit.
Row 2 Purl.
Row 3 * (P2tog) twice, (yo, k1) 3 times, yo, (p2tog) twice; rep from * to end.
Row 4 Purl.
Repeat these 4 rows.

Norwegian Fir

Multiple of 12 sts plus 1.
Row 1 (RS) P1, * p3, k5, p4; rep from * to end.
Row 2 and every foll WS row Purl.
Row 3 P2tog, * p2, k2, yo, k1, yo, k2, p2, p3tog; rep from * to end, ending last rep with p2tog.
Row 5 P2tog, * p1, k2, yo, k3, yo, k2, p1, p3tog; rep from * to end, ending last rep with p2tog.
Row 7 P2tog, * k2, yo, k5, yo, k2, p3tog; rep from * to end, ending last rep with p2tog.
Row 8 Purl.
Repeat these 8 rows.

Dainty Chevron

Multiple of 8 sts plus 1.
Row 1 (RS) K1, * ssk, (k1, yo) twice, k1, k2tog, k1; rep from * to end.
Row 2 and every foll WS row Purl.
Row 3 As row 1.
Row 5 K1, * yo, ssk, k3, k2tog, yo, k1; rep from * end.
Row 7 K1, * k1, yo, ssk, k1, k2tog, yo, k2; rep from * to end.
Row 9 K1, * k2, yo, sl2tog-k1-psso, yo, k3; rep from * to end.
Row 10 Purl.
Repeat these 10 rows.

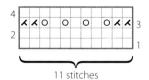

11 stitches

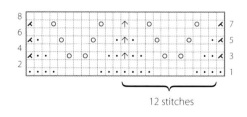

12 stitches

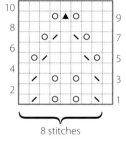

8 stitches

KEY

O	yo
/	k2tog
\	ssk
▲	sl2tog-k1-psso
⅄	p2tog
↑	p3tog
•	p on RS rows, k on WS rows
□	k on RS rows, p on WS rows

LACE STITCHES

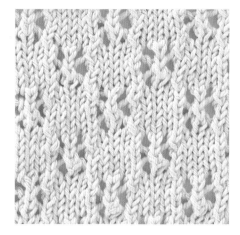

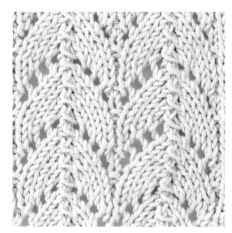

Snowflake Eyelets

Multiple of 8 sts plus 5.
Row 1 (RS) K1, * k3, ssk, yo, k1, yo, k2tog; rep from * to last 4 sts, k4.
Row 2 and every foll WS row Purl.
Row 3 K1, * k4, yo, sl2tog-k1-psso, yo, k1; rep from * to last 4 sts, k4.
Row 5 As row 1.
Row 7 Ssk, * yo, k1, yo, k2tog, k3, ssk; rep from * to last 3 sts, yo, k1, yo, k2tog.
Row 9 K1, * yo, sl2tog-k1-psso, yo, k5; rep from * to last 4 sts, yo, sl2tog-k1-p2sso, yo, k1.
Row 11 As row 7.
Row 12 Purl.
Repeat these 12 rows.

Mini Horseshoe Lace

Multiple of 6 sts plus 1.
Row 1 (RS) K1, * yo, k1, sk2po, k1, yo, k1; rep from * to end.
Row 2 Purl.
Row 3 K1, * k1, yo, sk2po, yo, k2; rep from * to end.
Row 4 Purl.
Repeat these 4 rows.

Horseshoe Lace

Multiple of 10 sts plus 1.
Row 1 (RS) K1, * yo, k3, sk2po, k3, yo, k1; rep from * to end.
Row 2 Purl.
Row 3 P1, * k1, yo, k2, sk2po, k2, yo, k1, p1; rep from * to end.
Row 4 K1, * p9, k1; rep from * to end.
Row 5 P1, * k2, yo, k1, sk2po, k1, yo, k2, p1; rep from * to end.
Row 6 As row 4.
Row 7 P1, * k3, yo, sk2po, yo, k3, p1; rep from * to end.
Row 8 Purl.
Repeat these 8 rows.

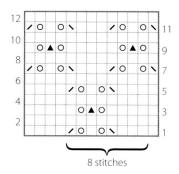

8 stitches

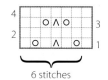

6 stitches

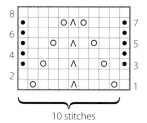

10 stitches

KEY

O	yo
/	k2tog
\	ssk
∧	sk2po
•	p on RS rows, k on WS rows
☐	k on RS rows, p on WS rows

LACE STITCHES

Diamonds

Multiple of 8 sts plus 1.
Row 1 (RS) K1, * k1, k2tog, yo, k1, yo, ssk, k2; rep from * to end.
Row 2 and every foll WS row Purl.
Row 3 K1, * k2tog, yo, k3, yo, ssk, k1; rep from * to end.
Row 5 K2tog, * yo, k5, yo, sk2po; rep from * to end, ending last rep with ssk.
Row 7 K1, * yo, ssk, k3, k2tog, yo, k1; rep from * to end.
Row 9 K1, * k1, yo, ssk, k1, k2tog, yo, k2; rep from * to end.
Row 11 K1, * k2, yo, sk2po, yo, k3; rep from * to end.
Row 12 Purl.
Repeat these 12 rows.

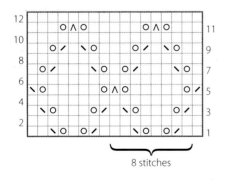

8 stitches

Leaf Patterned Lace

Multiple of 10 sts plus 1.
Row 1 (RS) K1, * k2, k2tog, yo, k1, yo, ssk, k3; rep from * to end.
Row 2 and every foll WS row Purl.
Row 3 K1, * k1, k2tog, (k1, yo) twice, k1, ssk, k2; rep from * to end.
Row 5 K1, * k2tog, k2, yo, k1, yo, k2, ssk, k1; rep from * to end.
Row 7 K2tog, * k3, yo, k1, yo, k3, sk2po; rep from * to end, ending last rep with ssk.
Row 9 K1, * yo, ssk, k5, k2tog, yo, k1; rep from * to end.
Row 11 K1, * yo, k1, ssk, k3, k2tog, k1, yo, k1; rep from * to end.
Row 13 K1, * yo, k2, ssk, k1, k2tog, k2, yo, k1; rep from * to end.
Row 15 K1, * yo, k3, sk2po, k3, yo, k1; rep from * to end.
Row 16 Purl.
Repeat these 16 rows.

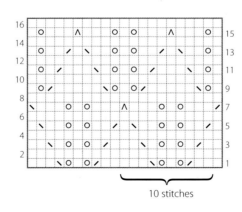

10 stitches

Ladder Lace

Multiple of 14 sts plus 11.
Row 1 (RS) K2tog, k3, yo, * k1, yo, k3, ssk, yo, sk2po, yo, k2tog, k3, yo; rep from * to last 6 sts, k1, yo, k3, ssk.
Row 2 Purl.
Repeat these 2 rows.

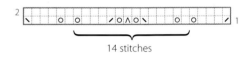

14 stitches

KEY

O	yo
╱	k2tog
╲	ssk
∧	sk2po
·	p on RS rows, k on WS rows
☐	k on RS rows, p on WS rows

LACE STITCHES

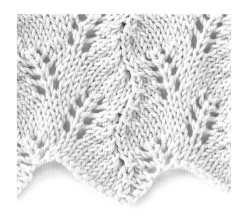

Fern Lace

Multiple of 16 sts.
Row 1 (RS) * K9, yo, k1, yo, k3, sk2po; rep
from * to end.
Row 2 and every foll WS row Purl.
Row 3 * K10, yo, k1, yo, k2, sk2po; rep from
* to end.
Row 5 * K3tog, k4, yo, k1, yo, k3,
(yo, k1) twice, sk2po; rep from * to end.
Row 7 * K3tog, k3, yo, k1, yo, k9; rep from
* to end.
Row 9 * K3tog, k2, yo, k1, yo, k10; rep from
* to end.
Row 11 * K3tog, (k1, yo) twice, k3, yo, k1,
yo, k4, sk2po; rep from * to end.
Row 12 Purl.
Repeat these 12 rows.

Beech Leaf Lace

Multiple of 14 sts plus 1 (stitch count
varies).
Row 1 (RS) K1, * yo, k5, yo, sk2po, yo, k5,
yo, k1; rep from * to end. 16 sts.
Row 2 Purl.
Row 3 K1, * yo, k1, k2tog, p1, ssk, k1, yo,
p1, yo, k1, k2tog, p1, ssk, k1, yo, k1; rep
from * to end.
Row 4 * P4, (k1, p3) 3 times; rep from * to
last st, p1.
Row 5 K1, * yo, k1, k2tog, p1, ssk, k1, p1,
k1, k2tog, p1, ssk, k1, yo, k1; rep from * to
end. 14 sts.
Row 6 * P4, k1, p2, k1, p2, k1, p3; rep from
* to last st, p1.
Row 7 K1, * yo, k1, yo, k2tog, p1, ssk, p1,
k2tog, p1, ssk, (yo, k1) twice; rep from *
to end.
Row 8 * P5, (k1, p1) twice, k1, p4; rep from
* to last st, p1.
Row 9 K1, * yo, k3, yo, sk2po, k1, k3tog, yo,
k3, yo, k1; rep from * to end.
Row 10 Purl.
Repeat these 10 rows.

Twin Leaf Lace

Multiple of 18 sts plus 1.
Row 1 (RS) P1, * k4, k3tog, yo, k1, yo, p1,
yo, k1, yo, sk2po, k4, p1; rep from * to end.
Row 2 and every foll WS row * K1, p8; rep
from * to last st, k1.
Row 3 P1, * k2, k3tog, (k1, yo) twice, k1,
p1, k1, (yo, k1) twice, sk2po, k2, p1; rep
from * to end.
Row 5 P1, * k3tog, k2, yo, k1, yo, k2, p1, k2,
yo, k1, yo, k2, sk2po, p1; rep from * to end.
Row 6 As row 2.
Repeat these 6 rows.

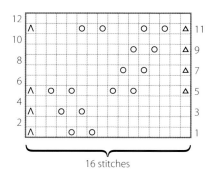

16 stitches

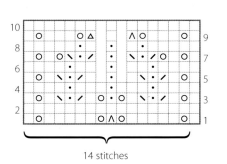

14 stitches

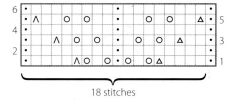

18 stitches

KEY

o	yo
╱	k2tog
╲	ssk
▵	k3tog
∧	sk2po
•	p on RS rows, k on WS rows
☐	k on RS rows, p on WS rows

LACE STITCHES

Diamond Lace with Rosettes

Multiple of 14 sts plus 3.

Row 1 (RS) K1, yo, * k3tog, yo, k9, yo, ssk, yo; rep from * to last 2 sts, k2tog.

Row 2 and every foll WS row Purl.

Row 3 K1, k2tog, * yo, k11, yo, sk2po; rep from * to end, ending last rep with ssk, k1.

Row 5 K2, * (yo, ssk) twice, k5, (k2tog, yo) twice, k1; rep from * to last st, k1.

Row 7 K2, * k1, (yo, ssk) twice, k3, (k2tog, yo) twice, k2; rep from * to last st, k1.

Row 9 K2, * k2, (yo, ssk) twice, k1, (k2tog, yo) twice, k3; rep from * to last st, k1.

Row 11 K2, * k3, yo, ssk, yo, sk2po, yo, k2tog, yo, k4; rep from * to last st, k1.

Row 13 K2, * k4, k2tog, yo, k1, yo, ssk, k5; rep from * to last st, k1.

Row 15 K2, * k3, k2tog, yo, k3, yo, ssk, k4; rep from * to last st, k1.

Row 17 K2, * k4, yo, ssk, yo, k3tog, yo, k5; rep from * to last st, k1.

Row 19 K2, * k5, yo, sk2po, yo, k6; rep from * to last st, k1.

Row 21 K2, * k2, (k2tog, yo) twice, k1, (yo, ssk) twice, k3; rep from * to last st, k1.

Row 23 K2, * k1, (k2tog, yo) twice, k3, (yo, ssk) twice, k2; rep from * to last st, k1.

Row 25 K2, * (k2tog, yo) twice, k5, (yo, ssk) twice, k1; rep from * to last st, k1.

Row 27 K1, k2tog, * yo, k2tog, yo, k7, yo, ssk, yo, sk2po; rep from * to end, ending last rep with ssk, k1.

Row 29 K2, * yo, ssk, k9, k2tog, yo, k1; rep from * to last st, k1.

Row 31 K2, * k1, yo, ssk, k7, k2tog, yo, k2; rep from * to last st, k1.

Row 32 Purl.

Repeat these 32 rows.

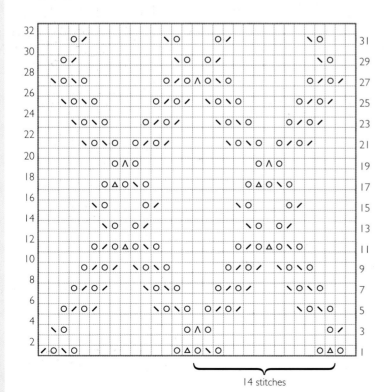

14 stitches

KEY

O	yo
╱	k2tog
╲	ssk
△	k3tog
∧	sk2po
·	p on RS rows, k on WS rows
☐	k on RS rows, p on WS rows

LACE STITCHES

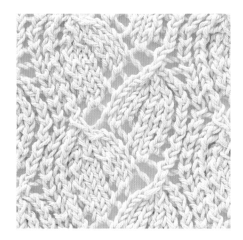

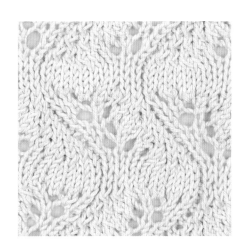

Dayflower

Multiple of 16 sts plus 1 (stitch count varies).
Row 1 (RS) K1, * yo, k2tog, yo, (k2tog) 3 times, k2, yo, k3, yo, ssk, yo, k1; rep from * to end.
Row 2 Purl.
Row 3 K1, * yo, k2tog, (k3tog) twice, yo, k1, yo, k2, (ssk, yo) twice, k1; rep from * to end. 15 sts.
Row 4 * P10, p2tog, p2; rep from * to last st, p1. 14 sts.
Row 5 K1, * yo, k3tog, yo, k3, yo, k2, (ssk, yo) twice, k1; rep from * to end. 15 sts.
Row 6 Purl.
Row 7 K1, * yo, k2tog, yo, k1, yo, k2, ssk, yo, k2, (ssk, yo) twice, k1; rep from * to end. 17 sts.
Row 8 Purl.

Row 9 K1, * yo, k2tog, yo, k3, yo, k2, (ssk) 3 times, yo, ssk, yo, k1; rep from * to end.
Row 10 Purl.
Row 11 K1, * (yo, k2tog) twice, k2, yo, k1, yo, (sk2po) twice, ssk, yo, k1; rep from * to end. 15 sts.
Row 12 * P3, p2tog tbl, p9; rep from * to last st, p1. 14 sts.
Row 13 K1, * (yo, k2tog) twice, k2, yo, k3, yo, sk2po, yo, k1; rep from * to end. 15 sts.
Row 14 Purl.
Row 15 K1, * (yo, k2tog) twice, k2, yo, k2tog, k2, yo, k1, yo, ssk, yo, k1; rep from * to end. 17 sts.
Row 16 Purl.
Repeat these 16 rows.

Japanese Feather

Multiple of 11 sts plus 1.
Row 1 (RS) P1, * k10, p1; rep from * to end.
Row 2 and every foll WS row * K1, p10; rep from * to last st, k1.
Row 3 As row 1.
Row 5 P1, * k1, (yo, k1) 3 times, (ssk) 3 times, p1; rep from * to end.
Row 7 P1, * k1, (k1, yo) 3 times, (ssk) 3 times, p1; rep from * to end.
Row 9 As row 5.
Row 11 As row 7.
Row 13 As row 5.
Row 15 As row 1.
Row 17 As row 1.
Row 19 P1, * (k2tog) 3 times, (k1, yo) 3 times, k1, p1; rep from * to end.

Row 21 P1, * (k2tog) 3 times, (yo, k1) 3 times, k1, p1; rep from * to end.
Row 23 As row 19.
Row 25 As row 21.
Row 27 As row 19.
Row 28 * K1, p10; rep from * to last st, k1.
Repeat these 28 rows.

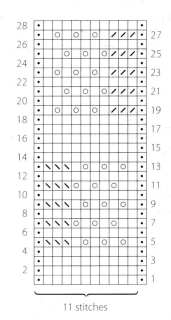

11 stitches

KEY

o	yo
∕	k2tog
＼	ssk
	p on RS rows, k on WS rows
□	k on RS rows, p on WS rows

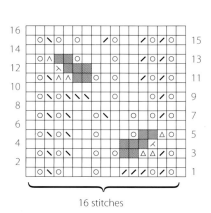

16 stitches

KEY

o	yo
∕	k2tog
＼	ssk
∧	sk2po
△	k3tog
⋋	p2tog
⋌	p2tog tbl
□	k on RS rows, p on WS rows
▨	no stitch

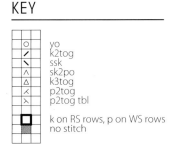

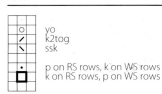

LACE STITCHES

Old Shale Pattern

Multiple of 18 sts plus 1.
Row 1 (RS) K1, * (k2tog) 3 times, (yo, k1) 5 times, yo, (k2tog) 3 times, k1; rep from * to end.
Row 2 Knit.
Row 3 Knit.
Row 4 Purl.
Repeat these 4 rows.

Fan and Feather Stitch

Multiple of 14 sts plus 1.
Row 1 (RS) K1 * k4tog, (yo, k1) 5 times, yo, k4tog tbl, k1; rep from * to end.
Row 2 * K4, p7, k3; rep from * to last st, k1.
Row 3 Knit.
Row 4 Purl.
Repeat these 4 rows.

Mrs Hunter's Pattern

Multiple of 4 sts plus 2.
Row 1 (RS) Knit.
Row 2 Purl.
Row 3 K1, * sl 1, k3, pass sl st over the k3; rep from * to last st, k1.
Row 4 P1, * p3, yo; rep from * to last st, p1.
Repeat these 4 rows.

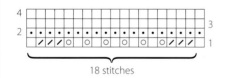

18 stitches

14 stitches

4 stitches

KEY

o	yo
/	k2tog
•	p on RS rows, k on WS rows
☐	k on RS rows, p on WS rows

KEY

o	yo
◢	k4tog
◣	k4tog tbl
•	p on RS rows, k on WS rows
☐	k on RS rows, p on WS rows

KEY

o	yo
s	slip st
	k3, pass sl st over
☐	k on RS rows, p on WS rows

LACE STITCHES

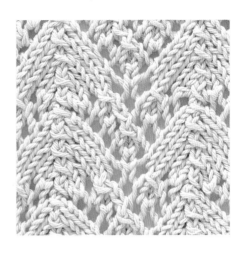

Field of Wheat

Abbreviation:
MB – (k1, yo, k1, yo, k1) into next st, turn and k5, turn and p5, turn and k1, sk2po, k1, turn and p3tog.

Multiple of 11 sts (stitch count varies).
Row 1 (RS) * K1, MB, k2, yo, k1, yo, k4, k2tog; rep from * to end. 12 sts.
Row 2 * P2tog, p10. 11 sts.
Row 3 * K5, yo, k1, yo, k3, k2tog; rep from * to end. 12 sts.
Row 4 As row 2.
Row 5 * K6, yo, k1, yo, k2, k2tog; rep from * to end. 12 sts.
Row 6 As row 2.
Row 7 * K7, (yo, k1) twice, k2tog; rep from * to end. 12 sts.

Row 8 As row 2.
Row 9 * K8, yo, k1, yo, k2tog; rep from * to end. 12 sts.
Row 10 As row 2.
Row 11 *Ssk, k4, yo, k1, yo, k2, MB, k1; rep from * to end. 12 sts.
Row 12 * P10, p2tog tbl; rep from * to end. 11 sts.
Row 13 *Ssk, k3, yo, k1, yo, k5; rep from * to end. 12 sts.
Row 14 As row 12.
Row 15 * Ssk, k2, yo, k1, yo, k6; rep from * to end. 12 sts.
Row 16 As row 12.
Row 17 * Ssk, (k1, yo) twice, k7; rep from * to end. 12 sts.
Row 18 As row 12.
Row 19 * Ssk, yo, k1, yo, k8; rep from * to end. 12 sts.
Row 20 As row 12.
Repeat these 20 rows.

Fan Pattern

Multiple of 12 sts plus 3.
Row 1 (RS) K1 * k1, yo, k4, sk2po, k4, yo; rep from * to last 2 sts, k2.
Row 2 and every foll WS row Purl.
Row 3 K1, * k2, yo, k3, sk2po, k3, yo, k1; rep from * to last 2 sts, k2.
Row 5 K1, k2tog, * yo, k1, yo, k2, sk2po, k2, yo, k1, yo, sk2po; rep from * to last 12 sts, yo, k1, yo, k2, sk2po, k2, yo, k1, yo, ssk, k1.

Row 7 K1, * yo, ssk, k2, yo, k1, sk2po, k1, yo, k3; rep from * to last 2 sts, yo, ssk.
Row 9 K1, * k1, yo, sk2po, yo; rep from * to last 2 sts, k2.
Row 10 Purl.
Repeat these 10 rows.

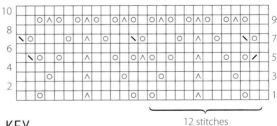

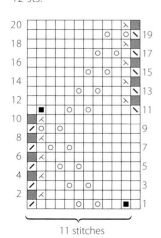
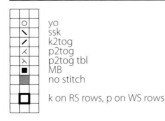

11 stitches

LACE STITCHES

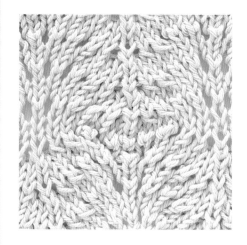

Ostrich Plumes

Multiple of 16 sts plus 1.

Row 1 K1, * (yo, k1) twice, yo, (ssk) twice, sl2tog-k1-psso, (k2tog) twice, (yo, k1) 3 times; rep from * to end.

Row 2 and every foll WS row Purl.

Row 3 Knit.

Row 5 As row 1.

Row 7 Knit.

Row 9 As row 1.

Row 11 Knit.

Row 13 As row 1.

Row 15 Knit.

Row 17 (K2tog) 3 times, * (yo, k1) 5 times, yo, (ssk) twice, sl2tog-k1-psso, (k2tog) twice; rep from * to last 11 sts, (yo, k1) 5 times, yo, (ssk) 3 times.

Row 19 Knit.

Row 21 As row 17.

Row 23 Knit.

Row 25 As row 17.

Row 27 Knit.

Row 29 As row 17.

Row 31 Knit.

Row 32 Purl.

Repeat these 32 rows.

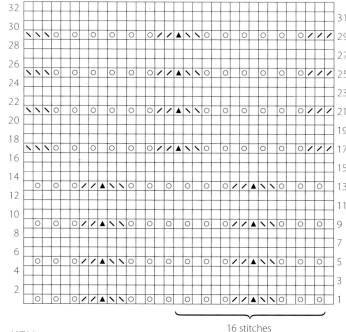

16 stitches

KEY

o	yo
╱	k2tog
╲	ssk
▲	sl2tog-k1-psso
□	k on RS rows, p on WS rows

LACE PANELS

Swiss Fan

Panel of 9 sts (stitch count varies).
Foundation Row (WS) K1, p7, k1.
Row 1 (RS) P1, ssk, (yo, k1) 3 times, yo, k2tog, p1. 11 sts.
Row 2 K1, p9, k1.
Row 3 P1, ssk, k5, k2tog, p1. 9 sts.
Row 4 K1, p7, k1.
Repeat these 4 rows.

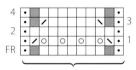

Panel of 9 stitches

KEY

O	yo
/	k2tog
\	ssk
•	p on RS rows, k on WS rows
□	k on RS rows, p on WS rows
	no stitch

Leaf Shadows

Panel of 19 sts (stitch count varies).
Row 1 (RS) Ssk, yo, k5, (yo, k1) 5 times, yo, k5, yo, k2tog. 25 sts.
Row 2 and every foll WS row Purl.
Row 3 Ssk, yo, ssk, k1, (k2tog, yo) twice, k3, yo, k1, yo, k3, (yo, ssk) twice, k1, k2tog, yo, k2tog. 25 sts.
Row 5 Ssk, yo, sl2tog-k1-psso, yo, k2tog, yo, k5, yo, k1, yo, k5, yo, ssk, yo, sl2tog-k1-psso, yo, k2tog. 25 sts.
Row 7 Sk2po, yo, k2tog, yo, k1, yo, ssk, k1, k2tog, yo, sl2tog-k1-psso, yo, ssk, k1, k2tog, yo, k1, yo, ssk, yo, k3tog. 21 sts.
Row 9 K1, k2tog, yo, k3, (yo, sl2tog-k1-psso) 3 times, yo, k3, yo, ssk, k1. 19 sts.
Row 10 Purl.
Repeat these 10 rows.

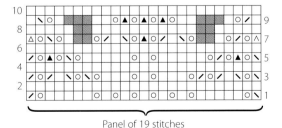

Panel of 19 stitches

KEY

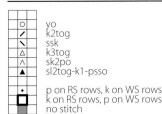

O	yo
/	k2tog
\	ssk
△	k3tog
∧	sk2po
▲	sl2tog-k1-psso
•	p on RS rows, k on WS rows
□	k on RS rows, p on WS rows
	no stitch

Honeybee

Panel of 12 sts (stitch count varies).
Row 1 (RS) K4, k2tog, yo, ssk, k4. 11 sts.
Row 2 P3, p2tog tbl, drop the yo off the needle, (yo) twice, p2tog, p3. 10 sts.
Row 3 K2, k2tog, drop the yos off the needle, (yo) 3 times, ssk, k2. 9 sts.
Row 4 P1, p2tog tbl, drop the yos off the needle, (yo) 4 times, p2tog, p1. 8 sts.
Row 5 K2tog, drop the yos off the needle, turn work and cast on 4 sts, turn work, insert RH needle under 4 loose strands, yarn round needle and pull loop through under loose strands, yo, insert RH needle under 4 loose strands, yarn round needle and pull loop through under loose strands, turn work and cast on 4 sts, turn work, ssk. 13 sts.
Row 6 P5, p2tog (st and following yo), p6. 12 sts.
Repeat these 6 rows.

LACE PANELS

Lacy Cable

Panel of 16 sts.
Row 1 (RS) P1, k1, yo, ssk, p1, k6, p1, k2tog, yo, k1, p1.
Row 2 K1, p3, k1, p6, k1, p3, k1.
Row 3 As row 1.
Row 4 As row 2.
Row 5 P1, k1, yo, ssk, p1, yo, work 6 cable sts as follows: (k3, yo, k3, pass first 3 sts of cable over 4 sts just worked), yo, p1, k2tog, yo, k1, p1.
Row 6 As row 2.
Repeat these 6 rows.

Veined Leaf

Panel of 9 sts (stitch count varies).
Foundation Row (WS) K3, p3, k3.
Row 1 P3, (k1, yo) twice, k1, p3. 11 sts.
Row 2 K3, p5, k3.
Row 3 P3, k2, yo, k1, yo, k2, p3. 13 sts.
Row 4 K3, p7, k3.
Row 5 P3, ssk, (k1, yo) twice, k1, k2tog, p3.
Row 6 As row 4.
Row 7 P3, ssk, k3, k2tog, p3. 11 sts.
Row 8 As row 2.
Row 9 P3, ssk, k1, k2tog, p3. 9 sts.
Row 10 K3, p3, k3.
Row 11 P3, yo, sl2tog-k1-psso, yo, p3.
Row 12 As row 10.
Repeat these 12 rows.

Flower Panel

Abbreviation:
MB – (k1, p1, k1, p1, k1) all into next st, pass 2nd, 3rd, 4th and 5th sts over first.

Panel of 13 sts.
Row 1 (RS) P1, k4, k2tog, yo, k5, p1.
Row 2 and every foll WS row K1, p11, k1.
Row 3 P1, k3, k2tog, yo, k1, yo, ssk, k3, p1.
Row 5 P1, k2, k2tog, yo, k3, yo, ssk, k2, p1.
Row 7 P1, (k1, k2tog, yo) twice, k2, yo, ssk, k1, p1.
Row 9 P1, k3, k2tog, yo, k1, yo, ssk, k3, p1.
Row 11 P1, k2, k2tog, yo, k3, yo, ssk, k2, p1.
Row 13 P1, k5, MB, k5, p1.
Row 15 P1, (k3, MB) twice, k3, p1.
Row 17 As row 13.
Row 18 K1, p11, k1.
Repeat these 18 rows.

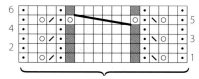

Panel of 16 stitches

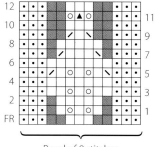

Panel of 9 stitches

KEY

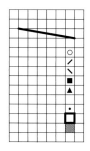

k3, yo, k3, pass first 3 sts over last 4 sts
o yo
/ k2tog
\ ssk
■ MB
▲ sl2tog-k1-psso
• p on RS rows, k on WS rows
□ k on RS rows, p on WS rows
   no stitch

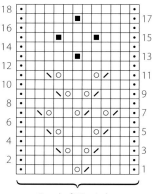

Panel of 13 stitches

EYELETS

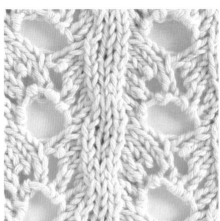

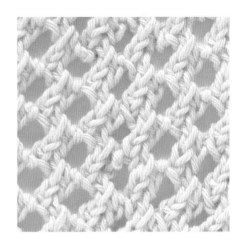

Cat's Paw

Multiple of 11 sts.
Row 1 (RS) * K3, k2tog, yo, k1, yo, ssk, k3; rep from * to end.
Row 2 and every foll WS row Purl.
Row 3 * K2, k2tog, yo, k3, yo, ssk, k2; rep from * to end.
Row 5 * K4, yo, sk2po, yo, k4; rep from * to end.
Row 6 Purl.
Repeat these 6 rows.

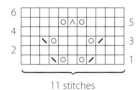

KEY

O	yo
/	k2tog
\	ssk
∧	sk2po
☐	k on RS rows, p on WS rows

Large Cat's Paw

Multiple of 14 sts plus 1 (stitch count varies).
Row 1 (RS) K1, * ssk, k9, k2tog, k1; rep from * to end. 13 sts.
Row 2 P1, * p2tog, p7, p2tog tbl, p1; rep from * to end. 11 sts.
Row 3 K1, * ssk, k2, (yo) 3 times, k3, k2tog, k1; rep from * to end. 12 sts.
Row 4 P1, * p2tog, p2, (k1, p1, k1, p1, k1) into 3 yos, p1, p2tog tbl, p1; rep from * to end.
Row 5 K1, * ssk, k6, k2tog, k1; rep from * to end. 10 sts.
Row 6 P1, * p2tog, p7; rep from * to end. 9 sts.
Row 7 K1, * k2, yo, k1, (yo) twice, k1, (yo) twice, k1, yo, k3; rep from * to end. 15 sts.
Row 8 P1, * p2, p into yo, p1, (k1, p1) into 2 yos, p1, (k1, p1) into 2 yos, p1, p into yo, p3; rep from * to end.
Repeat these 8 rows.

Cat's Eye

Multiple of 8 sts plus 4 (stitch count varies).
Row 1 (RS) K4, * (yo) twice, k4; rep from * to end. 16 sts.
Row 2 P2, p2tog, * (p1, k1) into 2 yo, (p2tog) twice; rep from * to last 6 sts, (p1, k1) into 2 yo, (p2tog) twice, p2. 12 sts.
Row 3 K2, yo,* k4, (yo) twice; rep from * to last 6 sts, k4, yo, k2. 15 sts.
Row 4 P2, p1 into yo, * (p2tog) twice, (p1, k1) into 2 yo; rep from * to last 7 sts, (p2tog) twice, p1 into yo, p2. 12 sts.
Repeat these 4 rows.

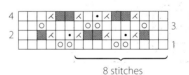

KEY

O	yo
⋌	p2tog
•	p on RS rows, k on WS rows
☐	k on RS rows, p on WS rows
▨	no stitch

EYELETS

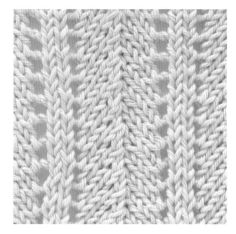

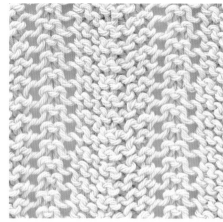

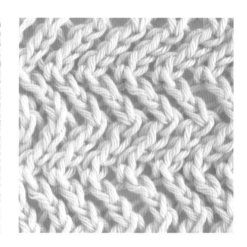

Razor Shell – st st version

Multiple of 11 sts plus 2.
Row 1 (RS) K2, * yo, k3, k3tog, k3, yo, k2;
rep from * to end.
Row 2 Purl.
Repeat these 2 rows.

Razor Shell – g st version

Multiple of 11 sts plus 2.
Row 1 (RS) K2, * yo, k3, k3tog, k3, yo, k2;
rep from * to end.
Row 2 Knit.
Repeat these 2 rows.

Zigzag Eyelets

Multiple of 4 sts plus 2.
Row 1 (RS) K1, * k2tog, yo; rep from * to
last st, k1.
Row 2 P2, * yo, p2tog; rep from * to end.
Row 3 As row 1.
Row 4 As row 2.
Row 5 K2, * yo, ssk; rep from * to end.
Row 6 P1, * p2tog tbl, yo; rep from * to
last st, p1.
Row 7 As row 5.
Row 8 As row 6.
Repeat these 8 rows.

4 stitches

KEY

○	yo
∕	k2tog
＼	ssk
⋋	p2tog
⋌	p2tog tbl
•	p on RS rows, k on WS rows
☐	k on RS rows, p on WS rows

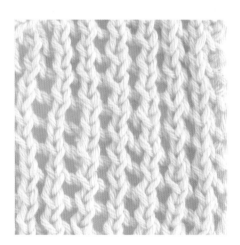

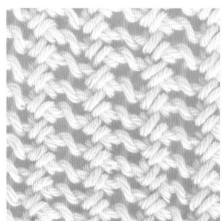

Trellis Mesh

Multiple of 2 sts plus 1.
Row 1 (RS) K1, * yo, k2tog; rep from *
to end.
Row 2 Purl.
Repeat these 2 rows.

Purse Stitch (reversible)

Multiple of 2 sts.
Row 1 P1, * yo, p2tog; rep from * to last
st, p1.
Repeat this row.

EYELETS

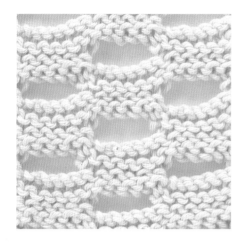

Open Buttonhole

Multiple of 12 sts plus 10.
Row 1 (RS) Knit.
Row 2 Knit.
Row 3 K8, * bind off 6 sts, k6 (including last st used in binding off); rep from * to last 2 sts, k2.
Row 4 K8, * cast on 6 sts, k6; rep from * to last 2 sts, k2.
Row 5 Knit.
Row 6 Knit.
Row 7 K2, * bind off 6 sts, k6 (including last st used in binding off); rep from * to last 8 sts, bind off 6 sts, k2 (including last st used in binding off).
Row 8 K2, * cast on 6 sts, k6; rep from * to last 8 sts, cast on 6 sts, k2.
Repeat these 8 rows.

Scroll Pattern

Multiple of 10 sts plus 2.
Row 1 (RS) K1, * yo, k8, k2tog; rep from * to last st, k1.
Row 2 P1, * p2tog, p7, yo, p1; rep from * to last st, p1.
Row 3 K1, * k2, yo, k6, k2tog; rep from * to last st, k1.
Row 4 P1, * p2tog, p5, yo, p3; rep from * to last st, p1.
Row 5 K1, * k4, yo, k4, k2tog; rep from * to last st, k1.
Row 6 P1, * p2tog, p3, yo, p5; rep from * to last st, p1.
Row 7 K1, * k6, yo, k2, k2tog; rep from * to last st, k1.
Row 8 P1, * p2tog, p1, yo, p7; rep from * to last st, p1.
Row 9 K1, * k8, yo, k2tog; rep from * to last st, k1.

Row 10 P1, * yo, p8, p2tog tbl; rep from * to last st, p1.
Row 11 K1, * ssk, k7, yo, k1; rep from * to last st, k1.
Row 12 P1, * p2, yo, p6, p2tog tbl; rep from * to last st, p1.
Row 13 K1, * ssk, k5, yo, k3; rep from * to last st, k1.
Row 14 P1, * p4, yo, p4, p2tog tbl; rep from * to last st, p1.
Row 15 K1, * ssk, k3, yo, k5; rep from * to last st, k1.
Row 16 P1, * p6, yo, p2, p2tog tbl; rep from * to last st, p1.
Row 17 K1, * ssk, k1, yo, k7; rep from * to last st, k1.
Row 18 P1, * p8, yo, p2tog tbl; rep from * to last st, p1.
Repeat these 18 rows.

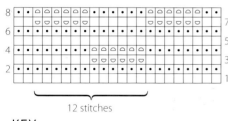

12 stitches

KEY

◡	cast off st
◠	cast on st
•	p on RS rows, k on WS rows
□	k on RS rows, p on WS rows

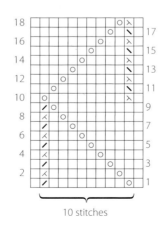

10 stitches

KEY

○	yo
╱	k2tog
╲	ssk
⅄	p2tog
⋋	p2tog tbl
□	p on RS rows, k on WS rows / k on RS rows, p on WS rows

DROP STITCH PATTERNS

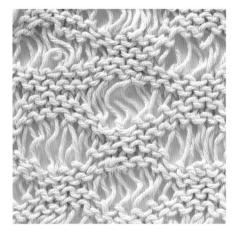

Seafoam

Multiple of 10 sts plus 6.
Row 1 (RS) Knit.
Row 2 Knit.
Row 3 K6, * yo twice, k1, yo 3 times, k1, yo 4 times, k1, yo 3 times, k1, yo twice, k6; rep from * to end.
Row 4 Knit to end, dropping all yos off needle.
Row 5 Knit.
Row 6 Knit.
Row 7 K1, * yo twice, k1, yo 3 times, k1, yo 4 times, k1, yo 3 times, k1, yo twice, k6; rep from * to end, ending last rep with k1 instead of k6.
Row 8 Knit to end, dropping all yos off needle.
Repeat these 8 rows.

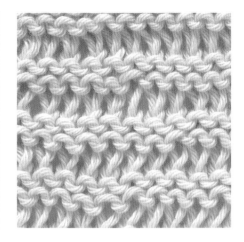

Bluebell Stitch

Multiple of 6 sts plus 2.
Row 1 (WS) Knit to end wrapping yarn twice round needle for each st.
Row 2 Knit to end working into first wrap only, dropping extra wraps off needle.
Row 3 K1, * p3tog, p2tog, pass 2nd st on RH needle over first st, (k1, p1, k1, p1, k1) into next st; rep from * to last st, k1.
Row 4 Purl.
Row 5 K1, * (k1, p1, k1, p1, k1) into next st, p3tog, p2tog, pass 2nd st on RH needle over first st; rep from * to last st, k1.
Row 6 Purl.
Repeat these 6 rows.

Long Garter Stitch

Any number of stitches.
Row 1 (RS) Knit.
Row 2 Knit.
Row 3 Knit to end wrapping yarn twice round needle for each st.
Row 4 Knit to end working into first wrap only, dropping extra wraps off needle.
Repeat these 4 rows.

Vertical Drop Stitch on Rev St St

Multiple of 8 sts plus 4 (stitch count varies).
Foundation Row (WS) K4, * yo, k8; rep from * to end. 13 sts.
Row 1 (RS) Purl.
Row 2 Knit.
Rep rows 1 and 2 twice more then row 1 again.
Row 8 K4, * drop next st off needle and unravel down to the yo 6 rows below, k4, yo, k4; rep from * to end.

Row 9 Purl.
Row 10 Knit.
Rep rows 9 and 10 twice more then row 9 again.
Row 16 K4, * yo, k4, drop next st off needle and unravel down ro 6 rows below, k4; rep from * to end.
Repeat these 16 rows.

DROP STITCH PATTERNS

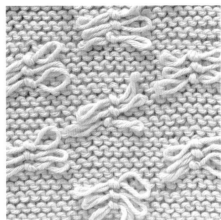

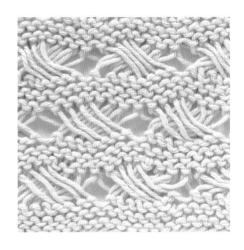

Vertical Drop Stitch Rib

Multiple of 8 sts plus 4 (stitch count varies).
Foundation Row (WS) K1, * p2, k1, yo, k1, p2, k2; rep from * to last 3 sts, p2, k1. 13 sts.
Row 1 (RS) P1, k2, * p2, k2, p3, k2; rep from * to last st, p1.
Row 2 K1, * p2, k3, p2, k2; rep from * to last 3 sts, p2, k1.
Rep rows 1 and 2 twice more then row 1 again.
Row 8 K1, * p2, k1, drop next st off needle and unravel down to the yo 6 rows below, k1, p2, k1, yo, k1; rep from * to last 3 sts, p2, k1.
Row 9 P1, k2, * p3, k2, p2, k2; rep from * to last st, p1.
Row 10 K1, * p2, k2, p2, k3; rep from * to last 3 sts, p2, k1.
Rep rows 9 and 10 twice more then row 9 again.
Row 16 K1, * p2, k1, yo, k1, p2, k1, drop next st off needle and unravel down to 6 rows below, k1; rep from * to last 3 sts, p2, k1.
Repeat these 16 rows.

Loop Bows

Multiple of 16 sts plus 9.
Row 1 (RS) Knit.
Row 2 K4, * (yo) 4 times, k1, (yo) 4 times, k15; rep from * to last 5 sts, (yo) 4 times, k1, (yo) 4 times, k4.
Row 3 K4, * drop 4 yos, k1, drop 4 yos, k15; rep from * to last 5 sts, drop 4 yos, k1, drop 4 yos, k4. Pull up each pair of loops and tie together into a knot.
Rep rows 2 and 3 twice more.
Row 8 Knit.
Row 9 Knit.
Row 10 K12, * (yo) 4 times, k1, (yo) 4 times, k15; rep from * to last 13 sts, (yo) 4 times, k1, (yo) 4 times, k12.
Row 11 K12, * drop 4 yos, k1, drop 4 yos, k15; rep from * to last 13 sts, drop 4 yos, k1, drop 4 yos, k12. Pull up each pair of loops and tie together into a knot.
Rep rows 10 and 11 twice more.
Row 16 Knit.
Repeat these 16 rows.

Indian Cross Stitch

Multiple of 8 sts.
Row 1 (WS) Knit.
Rows 2, 3 and 4 Knit.
Row 5 K to last st, wrapping yarn 4 times around needle for each st.
Row 6 * Sl 8 wyib, dropping all extra wraps, insert LH needle into first 4 of these 8 long sts and pass over the 2nd 4. Slip all 8 sts back to the LH needle and k each of these 8 sts; rep from * to end.
Rows 7, 8, 9 and 10 Knit.
Row 11 As row 5.
Row 12 Sl 4 wyib, dropping all extra wraps, insert LH needle into first 2 of these 4 long sts and pass over the 2nd 2. Slip all 4 sts back to LH needle and k each of these 4 sts, * sl 8 wyib, dropping all extra wraps, insert LH needle into first 4 of these 8 long sts and pass over the 2nd 4. Slip all 8 sts back to the LH needle and k each of these 8 sts; rep from * to last 4 sts, sl 4 wyib, dropping all extra wraps, insert LH needle into first 2 of these 4 long sts and pass over the 2nd 2. Slip all 4 sts back to LH needle and k each of these 4 sts.
Repeat these 12 rows.

DROP STITCH PATTERNS

Butterfly Drop Stitch

Abbreviation:

dropped dip st – insert RH needle from front to back through st 6 rows below next st on LH needle, drop next st off LH needle and unravel down to held st, place this held st and 5 loose strands on to LH needle, then knit it, catching the 5 loose strands in the st.

Multiple of 6 sts plus 1.
Foundation Row 1 (RS) Knit.
Foundation Row 2 Purl.
Row 1 Knit.
Row 2 Purl.
Repeat rows 1 and 2 once more.
Row 5 K3, * dropped dip st, k5; rep from * to last 4 sts, dropped dip st, k3.
Row 6 Purl.
Row 7 Knit.
Row 8 Purl.
Repeat rows 7 and 8 once more.
Row 11 K6, * dropped dip st, k5; rep from * to last 7 sts, dropped dip st, k6.
Row 12 Purl.
Repeat these 12 rows.

Ladder Check Stitch

Multiple of 11 sts plus 10.
Foundation Row (RS) P3, * yo, p2tog, p1, yo, p2tog, p6; rep from * to last 7 sts, yo, p2tog, p1, yo, p2tog, p2.
Row 1 Knit.
Row 2 Purl.
Row 3 Knit.
Row 4 Purl.
Row 5 Purl.
Row 6 Knit.
Row 7 Purl.
Row 8 Knit.
Repeat these 8 rows.
Finishing Row (WS) P3, * drop next st off needle, yo, p2, drop next st off needle, yo, p7; rep from * to last 7 sts, drop next st off needle, yo, p2, drop next st off needle, yo, p3.
Bind off. Unravel dropped sts.

Long Ladder and Cable

Abbreviation:

C4F – slip next 2 sts on to a cable needle at front of work, k2, then k2 from cable needle.

Multiple of 5 sts plus 1.
Foundation Row 1 K1, * p4, k1; rep from * to end.
Foundation Row 2 P1, * k3, ssk, yo; rep from * to last 5 sts, k4, p1.
Foundation Row 3 K1, p4, * k into yo, p4; rep from * to last st, k1.
Row 1 (RS) P1, * C4F, p1; rep from * to last 5 sts, k4, p1.
Row 2 * K1, p4; rep from * to last st, k1.
Row 3 P1, * k4, p1; rep from * to end.
Row 4 As row 2.
Repeat these 4 rows.
Finishing Row 1 P1, * C4F, drop next st off needle, yo; rep from * to last 5 sts, C4F, p1.
Finishing Row 2 K1, * p4, k1; rep from * to end.
Bind off. Unravel dropped sts.

EDGINGS

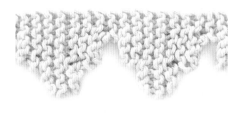

Loop Edging

Cast on 6 sts.
Row 1 (RS) K1, k2tog, yo, k2, (yo) twice, k1.
Row 2 K1, (k1, p1) into double yo, k5.
Row 3 K1, k2tog, yo, k5.
Row 4 Bind off 2 sts, p2tog, yo, k3.
Repeat these 4 rows.

Openwork Garter Stitch

Cast on 4 sts.
Row 1 (RS) K2, yfwd, k2.
Row 2 and every foll WS row Knit.
Row 3 K3, yfwd, k2.
Row 5 K2, yfwd, k2tog, yfwd, k2.
Row 7 K3, yfwd, k2tog, yfwd, k2.
Row 8 Bind off 4 sts, k to end.
Repeat these 8 rows.

Turret Edging

Cast on 3 sts.
Rows 1 to 3 Knit.
Row 4 Cast on 3 sts, k to end.
Rows 5 to 7 Knit.
Row 8 Cast on 3 sts, k to end.
Rows 9 to 11 Knit.
Row 12 Bind off 3 sts, k to end.
Rows 13 to 15 Knit.
Row 16 Bind off 3 sts, k to end.
Repeat these 16 rows.

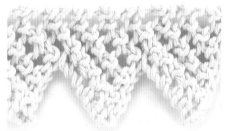

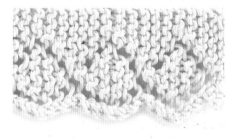

Scallop Border

Multiple of 13 sts.
Row 1 (RS) * K1, yo, k4, sk2po, k4, yo, k1;
rep from * to end.
Row 2 * P2, k9, p2; rep from * to end.
Row 3 * K2, yo, k3, sk2po, k3, yo, k2; rep
from * to end.
Row 4 * P3, k7, p3; rep from * to end.
Row 5 * K3, yo, k2, sk2po, k2, yo, k3; rep
from * to end.
Row 6 * P4, k5, p4; rep from * to end.
Row 7 * K4, yo, k1, sk2po, k1, yo, k4; rep
from * to end.
Row 8 * P5, k3, p5; rep from * to end.
Row 9 * K5, yo, sk2po, yo, k5; rep from *
to end.
Row 10 Purl.

Openwork Edging

Cast on 5 sts.
Row 1 (RS) Sl 1, yo, k2tog, yo, k2.
Row 2 and every foll WS row Knit.
Row 3 Sl 1, (yo, k2tog) twice, yo, k1.
Row 5 Sl 1, (yo, k2tog) twice, yo, k2.
Row 7 Sl 1, (yo, k2tog) 3 times, yo, k1.
Row 9 Sl 1, (yo, k2tog) 3 times, yo, k2.
Row 11 Bind off 6 sts, yo, k2tog, yo, k1.
Row 12 Knit.
Repeat these 12 rows.

Garter Stitch Diamond

Cast on 10 sts.
Row 1 (RS) K5, k2tog, yo, k3tog.
Row 2 and every foll WS row Yo,
k to end.
Row 3 K4, k2tog, yo, k1, yo, k2tog.
Row 5 K3, k2tog, yo, k3, yo, k2tog.
Row 7 K2, k2tog, yo, k5, yo, k2tog.
Row 9 K4, yo, k2tog, k1, k2tog, yo, k3tog.
Row 11 K5, yo, k3tog, yo, k3tog.
Row 12 Yo, k to end.
Repeat these 12 rows.

EDGINGS

Zig Zag Edging

Cast on 11 sts.
Row 1 (RS) K3, yo, k2tog, k2, yo, k2tog, yo, k2.
Row 2 Yo, k2tog, p8, k2.
Row 3 K2, (yo, k2tog) twice, k2, yo, k2tog, yo, k2.
Row 4 Yo, k2tog, p9, k2.
Row 5 K3, (yo, k2tog) twice, k2, yo, k2tog, yo, k2.
Row 6 Yo, k2tog, p10, k2.
Row 7 K2, (yo, k2tog) 3 times, k2, yo, k2tog, yo, k2.
Row 8 Yo, k2tog, p11, k2.
Row 9 K2, (ssk, yo) twice, k2, (ssk, yo) twice, k2tog, k1.
Row 10 Yo, k2tog, p10, k2.
Row 11 K1, (ssk, yo) twice, k2, (ssk, yo) twice, k2tog, k1.
Row 12 Yo, k2tog, p9, k2.
Row 13 K2, ssk, yo, k2, (ssk, yo) twice, k2tog, k1.
Row 14 Yo, k2tog, p8, k2.
Row 15 K1, ssk, yo, k2, (ssk, yo) twice, k2tog, k1.
Row 16 Yo, k2tog, p7, k2.
Repeat these 16 rows.

Leaf Edging

Cast on 6 sts.
Row 1 (RS) K3, yfwd, k1, yfwd, k2.
Row 2 P6, kf&b, k1.
Row 3 K2, p1, k2, yfwd, k1, yfwd, k3.
Row 4 P8, kf&b, k2.
Row 5 K2, p2, k3, yfwd, k1, yfwd, k4.
Row 6 P10, kf&b, k3.
Row 7 K2, p3, ssk, k5, k2tog, k1.
Row 8 P8, kf&b, p1, k3.
Row 9 K2, p1, k1, p2, ssk, k3, k2tog, k1.
Row 10 P6, kf&b, k1, p1, k3.
Row 11 K2, p1, k1, p3, ssk, k1, k2tog, k1.
Row 12 P4, kf&b, k2, p1, k3.
Row 13 K2, p1, k1, p4, sk2po, k1.
Row 14 P2tog, bind off 3 sts, k1, p1, k3.
Repeat these 14 rows.

Tassel Border

Multiple of 13 sts.
Row 1 (RS) * P2, (k1, p1) 4 times, k1, p2; rep from * to end.
Row 2 * K2, (p1, k1) 4 times, p1, k2; rep from * to end.
Rows 3 and 4 Repeat rows 1 and 2 once more.
Row 5 * P2, k1, p1, ssk, k1, k2tog, p1, k1, p2; rep from * to end.
Row 6 * K2, p1, k1, p3, k1, p1, k2; rep from * to end.
Row 7 * P2, k1, p1, sl2tog-k1-psso, p1, k1, p2; rep from * to end.
Row 8 * K2, (p1, k1) twice, p1, k2; rep from * to end.
Row 9 * P2, ssk, k1, k2tog, p2; rep from * to end.
Row 10 * K2, p3, k2; rep from * to end.
Row 11 * P2, sl next 3 sts on to cable needle, wrap yarn around them twice, k3 from cable needle, p2; rep from * to end.
Row 12 * K2, p3, k2; rep from * to end.
Row 13 * P1, sl2tog-k1-psso, p2; rep from * to end.
Row 14 Purl.
Repeat these 14 rows.

EDGINGS

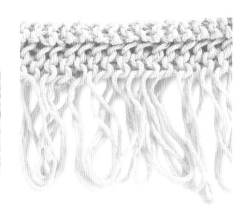

Welted Ruffle

Cast on 9 sts.
Row 1 Knit.
Row 2 P6 and turn, k6.
Row 3 P6, k3.
Row 4 K3, p6.
Row 5 K6 and turn, p6.
Row 6 Knit.
Repeat these 6 rows.

Cobweb Frill

Multiple of 3 sts plus 1.
Row 1 (RS) K1 tbl, * p1, p1 tbl, k1 tbl; rep from * to end.
Row 2 P1 tbl, * k1 tbl, k1, p1 tbl; rep from * to end.
Rows 3 to 8 Repeat rows 1 and 2 three times more.
Row 9 K1 tbl, * drop next st off needle, p1 tbl, k1 tbl; rep from * to end.
Row 10 P1 tbl, * k1 tbl, p1 tbl; rep from * to end.
Row 11 K1 tbl, * p1 tbl, k1 tbl; rep from * to end.
Rows 12 and 13 Repeat rows 10 and 11 once more.
Unravel dropped sts down to cast-on edge.

Fringe

Cast on 8 sts.
Row 1 (RS) K2, yo, k2tog, k4.
Row 2 P3, k2, yo, k2tog, k1.
Repeat these 2 rows for required length, ending with a WS row.
Last row Bind off 4 sts, draw yarn through next st and fasten off.
Slip rem 3 sts off needle and unravel.

EDGINGS

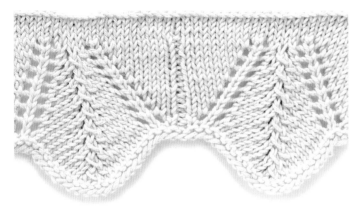

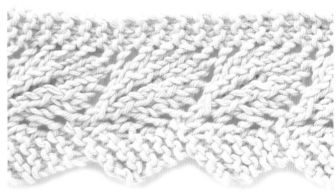

Fir Tree Border

Multiple of 26 sts plus 1.
Foundation Row (WS) Knit.
Row 1 P1, * k25, p1; rep from * to end.
Row 2 and every foll WS row K1, * p25, k1; rep from * to end.
Row 3 P1, * (k1, yo) twice, k7, ssk, sk2po, k2tog, k7, (yo, k1) twice, p1; rep from * to end.
Row 5 P1, * k2, yo, k1, yo, k6, ssk, sk2po, k2tog, k6, yo, k1, yo, k2, p1; rep from * to end.
Row 7 P1, * k3, yo, k1, yo, k5, ssk, sk2po, k2tog, k5, yo, k1, yo, k3, p1; rep from * to end.

Row 9 P1, * k4, yo, k1, yo, k4, ssk, sk2po, k2tog, k4, yo, k1, yo, k4, p1; rep from * to end.
Row 11 P1, * k5, yo, k1, yo, k3, ssk, sk2po, k2tog, k3, yo, k1, yo, k5, p1; rep from * to end.
Row 13 P1, * k6, yo, k1, yo, k2, ssk, sk2po, k2tog, k2, yo, k1, yo, k6, p1; rep from * to end.
Row 15 P1, * k7, (yo, k1) twice, ssk, sk2po, k2tog, (k1, yo) twice, k7, p1; rep from * to end.
Row 17 P1, * k8, yo, k1, yo, ssk, sk2po, k2tog, yo, k1, yo, k8, p1; rep from * to end.
Row 18 As row 2.

Birch Leaf Edging

Multiple of 13 sts (stitch count varies).
Row 1 (RS) K3, yo, k1, k2tog, p1, ssk, k1, yo, k3.
Row 2 K3, p3, k1, p3, k3.
Row 3 As row 1.
Row 4 As row 2.
Row 5 K3, yo, k1, yo, k2tog, p1, ssk, yo, k4. 14 sts.
Row 6 K4, p2, k1, p4, k3.
Row 7 (K3, yo) twice, sk2po, yo, k5. 15 sts.
Row 8 K5, p7, k3.
Row 9 K3, yo, k5, yo, k7. 17 sts.
Row 10 Bind off 4 sts, k3 (including last st used in binding off), p7, k3.
Repeat these 10 rows.

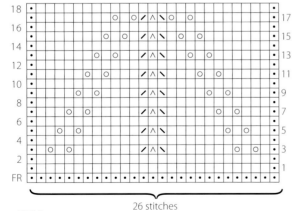

KEY

o	yo
/	k2tog
\	ssk
∧	sk2po
☐	p on RS rows, k on WS rows / k on RS rows, p on WS rows

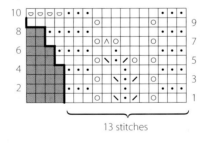

13 stitches

KEY

o	yo
/	k2tog
\	ssk
∧	sk2po
⌐	cast off
•	p on RS rows, k on WS rows
☐	k on RS rows, p on WS rows
	no stitch

EDGINGS

Lacy Leaf Edging

Cast on 31 sts.

Row 1 (RS) K1, yo, k2tog, yo, k3, yo, k2tog, p1, yo, p1, k2, yo, k2tog, p1, ssk, k5, k2tog, p1, k2, yo, k2tog, k2.

Row 2 K4, yo, k2tog, k1, p7, k3, yo, k2tog, k1, p1, k3, yo, k2tog, k5.

Row 3 K1, yo, k2tog, yo, k4, yo, k2tog, p1, yo, k1, yo, p1, k2, yo, k2tog, p1, k7, p1, k2, yo, k2tog, k2. 34 sts.

Row 4 K4, yo, k2tog, k1, p7, k3, yo, k2tog, k1, p3, k3, yo, k2tog, k6.

Row 5 K1, yo, k2tog, yo, k5, yo, k2tog, p1, (k1, yo) twice, k1, p1, k2, yo, k2tog, p1, ssk, k3, k2tog, p1, k2, yo, k2tog, k2. 35 sts.

Row 6 K4, yo, k2tog, k1, p5, k3, yo, k2tog, k1, p5, k3, yo, k2tog, k7.

Row 7 K1, yo, k2tog, yo, k6, yo, k2tog, p1, k2, yo, k1, yo, k2, p1, k2, yo, k2tog, p1, ssk, k1, k2tog, p1, k2, yo, k2tog, k2. 36 sts.

Row 8 K4, yo, k2tog, k1, p3, k3, yo, k2tog, k1, p7, k3, yo, k2tog, k8.

Row 9 K1, yo, k2tog, yo, k7, yo, k2tog, p1, k3, yo, k1, yo, k3, p1, k2, yo, k2tog, p1, sk2po, p1, k2, yo, k2tog, k2. 37 sts.

Row 10 K4, yo, k2tog, k1, p1, k3, yo, k2tog, k1, p9, k3, yo, k2tog, k9.

Row 11 K1, yo, k2tog, yo, k2, yo, k2tog, p2, k2, yo, k2tog, p1, k9, p1, k2, yo, k2tog, p1, k8. 38 sts.

Row 12 Bind off 4 sts, k4 (including last st used in casting off), pass first 3 of these 4 sts over last st worked, k3, yo, k2tog, k1, p9, k3, yo, k2tog, k4, yo, k2tog, k4. 31 sts.
Repeat these 12 rows.

Large Eyelet

Cast on 10 sts.

Foundation Row 1 K3, p7.

Foundation Row 2 K2, (yo) 4 times, k2tog, k3 and turn.

Foundation Row 3 P4, (k1, p1, k1, p1) into 4-yo loop, p2.

Row 1 (RS) K13.

Row 2 K3, p10.

Row 3 K2, (yo) 5 times, k2tog, k6 and turn.

Row 4 P7, (k1, p1, k1, p1, k1) into 5 yo loop, p2.

Row 5 K17.

Row 6 K3, p14.

Row 7 Bind off 7 sts, k2 (including last st used in binding off), (yo) 4 times, k2tog, k3 and turn.

Row 8 P4, (k1, p1, k1, p1) into 4 yo loop, p2.
Repeat these 8 rows.

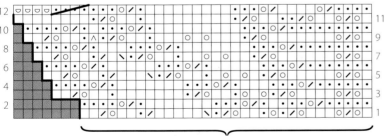

31 stitches

KEY

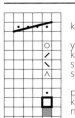

k4, pass first 3 sts over 4th

○ yo
╱ k2tog
╲ ssk
∧ sk2po

• p on RS rows, k on WS rows
□ k on RS rows, p on WS rows
▨ no stitch

EDGINGS

 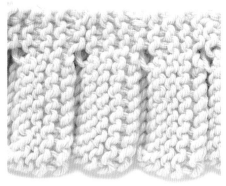 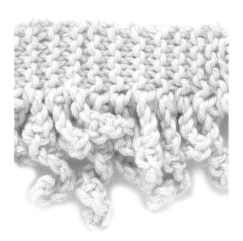

Shell Edging

Cast on 15 sts.
Row 1 (RS) K2, yo, p2tog, k7, yo, k2tog, k2.
Row 2 P11, yo, p2tog, k2.
Row 3 K2, yo, p2tog, k3, k2tog, k2, (yo, k2tog) twice. 14 sts.
Row 4 P10, yo, p2tog, k2.
Row 5 K2, yo, p2tog, k2, k2tog, k2, yo, k2tog, k2. 13 sts.
Row 6 P9, yo, p2tog, k2.
Row 7 K2, yo, p2tog, k1, k2tog, k2, (yo, k2tog) twice. 12 sts.
Row 8 P8, yo, p2tog, k2.
Row 9 K2, yo, p2tog, k2tog k2, yo, k1, yo, k3. 13 sts.
Row 10 As row 6.
Row 11 K2, yo, p2tog, k2tog, k1, yo, k3, yo, k1, yo, k2tog. 14 sts.
Row 12 As row 4.
Row 13 K2, yo, p2tog, k2tog, yo, k5, yo, k3. 15 sts.
Row 14 P11, yo, p2tog, k2.
Repeat these 14 rows.

Garter Stitch Loops

Cast on 26 sts.
Knit 6 rows.
Row 7 (RS) K3, bind off 20 sts, k to end.
Row 8 K3, cast on 20 sts, k to end.
Repeat these 8 rows, ending with row 6.
Fold in half and stitch long edges together to form loops.

Seaweed Fringe

Cast on 20 sts.
Foundation Row 1 Bind off 14 sts, k to end.
Foundation Row 2 K6.
Row 1 (RS) Cast on 10 sts, bind off 10 sts, k to end.
Row 2 and every foll WS row K6.
Row 3 Cast on 8 sts, bind off 8 sts, k to end.
Row 5 Cast on 12 sts, bind off 12 sts, k to end.
Row 7 Cast on 6 sts, bind off 6 sts, k to end.
Row 9 Cast on 8 sts, bind off 8 sts, k to end.
Row 11 Cast on 14 sts, bind off 14 sts, k to end.
Row 12 K6.
Repeat these 12 rows.

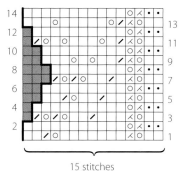

15 stitches

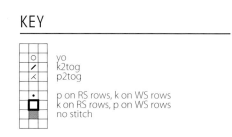

KEY

O	yo
╱	k2tog
⤢	p2tog
•	p on RS rows, k on WS rows
□	k on RS rows, p on WS rows
▨	no stitch

EDGINGS

Turret Border

Abbreviation:
MB – make a bobble by (k1, p1) twice into next st and turn, p4 and turn, k4 and turn, (p2tog) twice and turn, k2tog.

Cast on 3 sts.
Rows 1, 2 and 3 K3.
Row 4 Cast on 3 sts, p to end. 6 sts.
Rows 5, 6 and 7 K6.
Row 8 Cast on 3 sts, k to end. 9 sts.
Row 9 K9.
Row 10 P9.
Row 11 K7, MB, k1.
Row 12 P9.
Rows 13, 14 and 15 K9.
Row 16 Bind off 3 sts, k to end. 6 sts.
Row 17 K6.
Row 18 P6.
Row 19 K6.
Row 20 Bind off 3 sts, k to end. 3 sts.
Repeat these 20 rows.

Short Row Ruffle

Cast on 8 sts.
Rows 1 and 2 K6 and turn, k6.
Rows 3 and 4 K5 and turn, k5.
Rows 5 and 6 K4 and turn, k4.
Rows 7 and 8 K3 and turn, k3.
Rows 9 and 10 K2 and turn, k2.
Rows 11, 12, 13 and 14 K8.
Repeat these 14 rows.

Lace Ruffle

Cast on 4 sts.
Row 1 Knit.
Row 2 K2, * yo, k2; rep from * to end.
Row 3 Purl.
Row 4 K2, * yo, k1, yo, k2; rep from * to end.
Row 5 Purl.
Row 6 K2, * yo, k3, yo, k2; rep from * to end.
Row 7 Purl.
Row 8 K2, * yo, k5, yo, k2; rep from * to end.
Row 9 Purl.
Row 10 Purl.
Bind off purlwise.

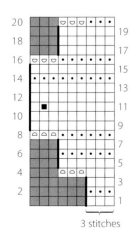

3 stitches

KEY

	Cast on
▫	
■	MB
•	p on RS rows, k on WS rows
☐	k on RS rows, p on WS rows
▨	no stitch

SLIP STITCH PATTERNS

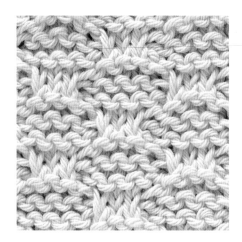

Slipped Basketweave

Multiple of 8 sts plus 5.
Row 1 (RS) Knit.
Row 2 K5, * sl 3 wyif, k5; rep from * to end.
Row 3 K5, * sl 3 wyib, k5; rep from * to end.
Row 4 As row 2.
Row 5 As row 3.
Row 6 As row 2.
Row 7 Knit.
Row 8 K1, * sl 3 wyif, K5; rep from * to last 4 sts, sl 3 wyif, k1.
Row 9 K1, * sl 3 wyib, K5; rep from * to last 4 sts, sl 3 wyib, k1.
Row 10 As row 8.
Row 11 As row 9.
Row 12 As row 8.
Repeat these 12 rows.

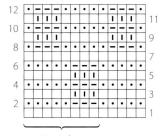

10 stitches

KEY

	sl 1 wyib
-	sl 1 wyif
·	p on RS rows, k on WS rows
□	k on RS rows, p on WS rows

Mock Honeycomb

Abbreviation:
gathering st – insert RH needle from below under the 2 loose strands, knit the next st, bringing the st out under the strands.

Multiple of 4 sts plus 1.
Foundation Row Purl.
Row 1 (RS) K1, * sl 3 wyif, k1; rep from * to end.
Row 2 P1, * sl 3 wyib, p1; rep from * to end.
Row 3 K2, * gathering st, k3; rep from * to last 3 sts, gathering st, k2.
Row 4 Purl.
Row 5 K3, * sl 3 wyif, k1; rep from * to last 2 sts, k2.
Row 6 P3, * sl 3 wyib, p1: rep from * to last 2 sts, k2.
Row 7 K4, * gathering st, k3; rep from * to last 2 sts, gathering st, k1.
Row 8 Purl.
Repeat these 8 rows.

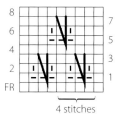

4 stitches

KEY

⋎	gathering st
		sl 1 wyib
-	sl 1 wyif
·	p on RS rows, k on WS rows
□	k on RS rows, p on WS rows

Mock Cable

Multiple of 7 plus 2.
Row 1 (RS) P2, * sl 1 wyif, k4, p2; rep from * to end.
Row 2 K2, * p3, sl 2 wyib, k2; rep from * to end.
Row 3 P2, * k1, sl 2 wyif, k2, p2; rep from * to end.
Row 4 K2, * p1, sl 2 wyib, p2, k2; rep from * to end.
Row 5 P2, * k3, sl 2 wyif, p2; rep from * to end.
Row 6 K2, * sl 1 wyib, p4, k2; rep from * to end.
Repeat these 6 rows.

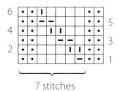

7 stitches

KEY

		sl 1 wyib
-	sl 1 wyif
·	p on RS rows, k on WS rows
□	k on RS rows, p on WS rows

SLIP STITCH PATTERNS

Butterfly Stitch

Abbreviation:
gathering st – insert RH needle from below under the 3 loose strands, purl next st on LH needle, pulling the loop through under the strands.

Multiple of 10 sts plus 7.
Row 1 (RS) K1, * k5, sl 5 wyif; rep from * to last 6 sts, k6.
Row 2 Purl.
Repeat rows 1 and 2 once more.
Row 5 As row 1.
Row 6 P8, * gathering st, p9; rep from * to last 9 sts, gathering st, p8.
Row 7 K1, * sl 5 wyif, k5; rep from * to last 6 sts, sl5 wyif, k1.
Row 8 Purl.
Repeat rows 7 and 8 once more.
Row 11 As row 7.
Row 12 P3, * gathering st, p9; rep from * to last 4 sts, gathering st, p3.
Repeat these 12 rows.

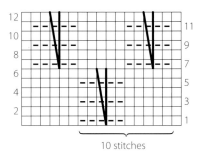

10 stitches

Heel Stitch

Odd number of sts.
Row 1 (RS) K1, * sl 1 wyib, k1; rep from * to end.
Row 2 Purl.
Repeat these 2 rows.

KEY

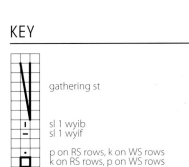

gathering st

| | sl 1 wyib
— | sl 1 wyif

· | p on RS rows, k on WS rows
☐ | k on RS rows, p on WS rows

Bowknot Stitch

Abbreviation:
gathering st - insert RH needle under 4 loose strands and through st below next st on LH needle from front to back, yarn round needle and pull a loop through, place loop on to LH needle, then k2tog tbl new loop and next st on LH needle.

Multiple of 6 sts plus 5.
Row 1 (Foundation Row) Knit.
Row 2 (WS) P4, * sl 3 wyib, p3; rep from * to last st, p1.
Row 3 K4, * sl 3 wyif, k3; rep from * to last st, k1.
Repeat rows 2 and 3 once more.
Row 6 Purl.
Row 7 K5, * gathering st, k5; rep from * to end.
Row 8 P1, * sl 3 wyib, p3; rep from * to last 4 sts, sl 3 wyib, p1.
Row 9 K1, * sl 3 wyif, k3; rep from * to last 4 sts, sl 3 wyif, k1.
Repeat rows 8 and 9 once more.
Row 12 Purl.
Row 13 K2, * gathering st, k5; rep from * to last 3 sts, gathering st, k2.
Repeat rows 2 to 13.

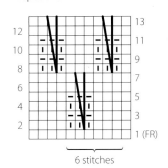

6 stitches

SLIP STITCH PATTERNS

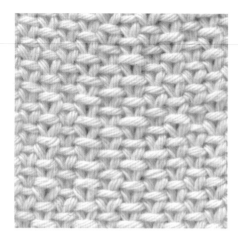

Woven Fabric

Odd number of stitches.
Row 1 (RS) K1, * sl 1 wyif, k1; rep from *
to end.
Row 2 P2, * sl 1 wyib, p1; rep from * to
last st, p1.
Repeat these 2 rows.

2 stitches

KEY

	sl 1 wyib
	sl 1 wyif
	p on RS rows, k on WS rows
	k on RS rows, p on WS rows

Herringbone Fabric

Multiple of 6 sts.
Row 1 (RS) * K3, sl 3 wyif; rep from *
to end.
Row 2 P1, * sl 3 wyib, p3; rep from * to last
5 sts, sl 3 wyib, p2.
Row 3 K1, * sl 3 wyif, k3; rep from * to last
5 sts, sl 3 wyif, k2.
Row 4 * P3, sl 3 wyib; rep from * to end.
Row 5 Sl 2 wyif, * k3, sl 3 wyif; rep from *
to last 4 sts, k3, sl 1 wyif.
Row 6 Sl 2 wyib, * p3, sl 3 wyib; rep from *
to last 4 sts, p3, sl 1 wyib.
Row 7 As row 1.
Row 8 As row 2.
Row 9 As row 3.
Row 10 As row 4.

Row 11 As row 1.
Row 12 Sl 2 wyib, * p3, sl 3 wyib; rep from
* to last 4 sts, p3, sl 1 wyib.
Row 13 Sl 2 wyif, * k3, sl 3 wyif; rep from *
to last 4 sts, k3, sl 1 wyif.
Row 14 * P3, sl 3 wyib; rep from * to end.
Row 15 K1, * sl 3 wyif, k3; rep from * to
last 5 sts, sl 3 wyif, k2.
Row 16 P1, * sl 3 wyib, p3; rep from * to
last 5 sts, sl 3 wyib, p2.
Row 17 * K3, sl 3 wyif; rep from * to end.
Row 18 As row 12.
Row 19 As row 13.
Row 20 As row 14.
Repeat these 20 rows.

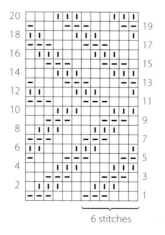

6 stitches

KEY

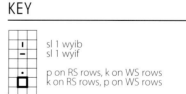

	sl 1 wyib
	sl 1 wyif
	p on RS rows, k on WS rows
	k on RS rows, p on WS rows

SLIP STITCH COLOUR PATTERNS

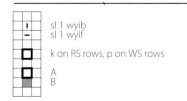

Houndstooth Check

Abbreviation:

dip st – insert RH needle from front to back through st in row below next st on LH needle, yarn round needle and draw through a loop, place loop on to LH needle, then k2tog tbl the new loop and next st on LH needle.

Multiple of 4 sts plus 2. Two colours A and B.
Foundation Row 1 Using A, knit.
Foundation Row 2 Using A, purl.
Row 1 (RS) Using B, k1, * sl 1 wyib, dip st, k2; rep from * to last st, k1.
Row 2 Using B, purl.
Row 3 Using A, k3, * sl 1 wyib, dip st, k2; rep from * to last 3 sts, sl 1 wyib, dip st, k1.
Row 4 Using A, purl.
Repeat these 4 rows.

French Weave

Multiple of 4 sts plus 3. Two colours A and B.
Foundation Row (WS) Using A, purl.
Row 1 (RS) Using B, k1, sl1 wyif, k1, * sl 1 wyib, k1, sl 1 wyif, k1; rep from * to end.
Row 2 Using B, p3, * sl 1 wyif, p3; rep from * to end.
Row 3 Using A, k1, * sl 1 wyif, k3; rep from * to last 2 sts, sl 1 wyif, k1.
Row 4 Using A, purl.
Row 5 Using B, k1, sl 1 wyib, k1, * sl 1 wyif, k1, sl 1 wyib, k1; rep from * to end.
Row 6 Using B, p1, * sl 1 wyif, p3; rep from * to last 2 sts, sl 1 wyif, p1.
Row 7 Using A, k3, * sl 1 wyif, k3; rep from * to end.
Row 8 Using A, purl.
Repeat these 8 rows.

Wave Stitch

Multiple of 6 sts plus 5. Two colours A and B.
Foundation Row 1 Using A, knit.
Foundation Row 2 Using A, purl.
Row 1 (RS) Using B, k1, * sl 3 wyib, k3; rep from * to last 4 sts, sl 3 wyib, k1.
Row 2 Using B, p2, * sl 1 wyif, p5; rep from * to last 3 sts, sl 1 wyif, p2.
Row 3 Using B, knit.
Row 4 Using B, purl.
Row 5 Using A, k4, * sl 3 wyib, k3; rep from * to last st, k1.
Row 6 Using A, p5, * sl 1 wyif, p5; rep from * to end.
Row 7 Using A, knit.
Row 8 Using A, purl.
Repeat these 8 rows.

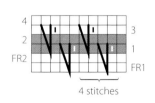

4 stitches

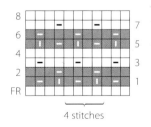

4 stitches

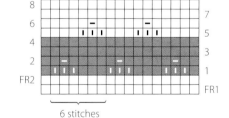

6 stitches

KEY

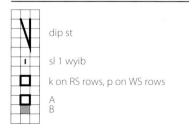

dip st

sl 1 wyib

k on RS rows, p on WS rows

A
B

KEY

sl 1 wyib
sl 1 wyif

k on RS rows, p on WS rows

A
B

KEY

sl 1 wyib
sl 1 wyif

k on RS rows, p on WS rows

A
B

SLIP STITCH COLOUR PATTERNS

Hexagon Pattern

Multiple of 8 sts plus 6. Two colours A and B.

Rows 1, 2, 3 and 4 Using A, knit.
Row 5 (RS) Using B, k2, * sl 2 wyib, k6; rep from * to last 4 sts, sl 2 wyib, k2.
Row 6 Using B, p2, * sl 2 wyif, p6; rep from * to last 4 sts, sl 2 wyif, p2.
Row 7 Using B, as row 5.
Row 8 Using B, as row 6.
Row 9 Using B, as row 5.
Row 10 Using B, as row 6.
Rows 11, 12, 13 and 14 Using A, knit.
Row 15 Using B, k6, * sl 2 wyib, k6; rep from * to end.
Row 16 Using B, p6, * sl 2 wyif, p6; rep from * to end.
Row 17 Using B, as row 15.
Row 18 Using B, as row 16.
Row 19 Using B, as row 15.
Row 20 Using B, as row 16.
Repeat these 20 rows.

Corn on the Cob Stitch

Multiple of 2 sts. Two colours A and B.
Foundation Row Using A, knit.
Row 1 (RS) Using B, k2, * sl 1 wyib, k1; rep from * to end.
Row 2 Using B, * k1, sl 1 wyif; rep from * to last 2 sts, k2.
Row 3 Using A, * k1, sl 1 wyib; rep from * to last 2 sts, k2.
Row 4 Using A, k2, * sl 1 wyif, k1; rep from * to end.
Repeat these 4 rows.

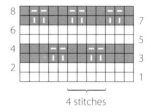

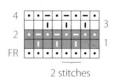

2 stitches

Simple Squares

Multiple of 4 sts. Two colours A and B.
Row 1 (RS) Using A, knit.
Row 2 Using A, purl.
Row 3 Using B, k3, * sl 2 wyib, k2; rep from * to last st, k1.
Row 4 Using B, p3, * sl 2 wyif, p2; rep from * to last st, p1.
Row 5 Using A, knit.
Row 6 Using A, purl.
Row 7 Using B, k1, * sl 2 wyib, k2; rep from * to last 3 sts, sl 2 wyib, k1.
Row 8 Using B, p1, * sl 2 wyif, p2; rep from * to last 3 sts, sl 2 wyif, p1.
Repeat these 8 rows.

4 stitches

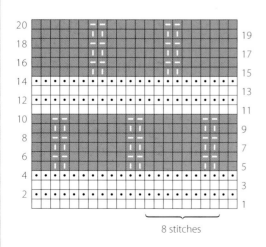

8 stitches

KEY

I	sl 1 wyib
–	sl 1 wyif
·	p on RS rows, k on WS rows
□	k on RS rows, p on WS rows
□	A
▨	B

SLIP STITCH COLOUR PATTERNS

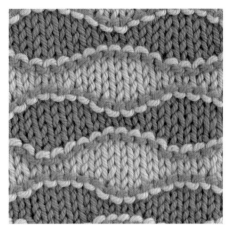

Three and One Tweed

Multiple of 4 sts plus 3. Two colours A and B.
Foundation Row Using B, knit.
Row 1 (RS) Using A, k3, * sl 1 wyib, k3; rep from * to end.
Row 2 Using A, k3, * sl 1 wyif, k3; rep from * to end.
Row 3 Using B, k1, * sl 1 wyib, k3; rep from * to last 2 sts, sl 1 wyib, k1.
Row 4 Using B, k1, * sl 1 wyif, k3; rep from * to last 2 sts, sl 1 wyif, k1.
Repeat these 4 rows.

Ripple Stitch

Multiple of 10 sts plus 3. Two colours A and B.
Foundation Row 1 (RS) Using A, knit.
Foundation Row 2 Using A, purl.
Row 1 (RS) Using A, knit.
Row 2 Using B, knit.
Row 3 Using B, k1, sl 1 wyib, k3, * sl 7 wyib, k3; rep from * to last 5 sts, sl 4 wyib, k1.
Row 4 Using B, p1, sl 3 wyif, p5, * sl 5 wyif, p5; rep from * to last 4 sts, sl 3 wyif, p1.
Row 5 Using B, k1, sl 2 wyib, k7, * sl 3

wyib, k7; rep from * to last 3 sts, sl 2 wyib, k1.
Row 6 Using B, purl.
Row 7 Using B, knit.
Row 8 Using A, knit.
Row 9 Using A, k3, * sl 7 wyib, k3; rep from * to end.
Row 10 Using A, p4, sl 5 wyif, * p5, sl 5 wyif; rep from * to last 4 sts, p4.
Row 11 Using A, k5, sl 3 wyib, * k7, sl 3 wyib; rep from * to last 5 sts, k5.
Row 12 Using A, purl.
Repeat these 12 rows.

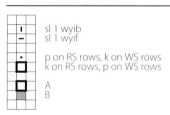

4 stitches

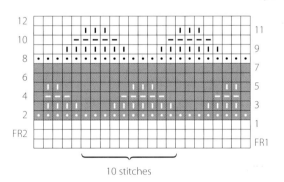

10 stitches

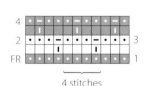

KEY

I	sl 1 wyib
−	sl 1 wyif
•	p on RS rows, k on WS rows
□	k on RS rows, p on WS rows
□	A
▨	B

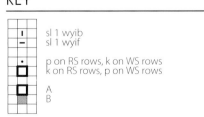

KEY

I	sl 1 wyib
−	sl 1 wyif
•	p on RS rows, k on WS rows
□	k on RS rows, p on WS rows
□	A
▨	B

SLIP STITCH COLOUR PATTERNS

Simple Vertical Stripes

Multiple of 4 sts. Two colours A and B.
Foundation Row Using B, purl.
Row 1 (RS) Using A, k1, * sl 2 wyib, k2; rep from * to last 3 sts, sl 2 wyib, k1.
Row 2 Using A, k1, * sl 2 wyif, p2; rep from * to last 3 sts, sl 2 wyif, k1.
Row 3 Using B, k1, * k2, sl 2 wyib; rep from * to last 3 sts, k3.
Row 4 Using B, k1, * p2, sl 2 wyif; rep from * to last 3 sts, p2, k1.
Repeat these 4 rows.

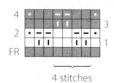

4 stitches

KEY

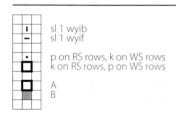

	sl 1 wyib
	sl 1 wyif
	p on RS rows, k on WS rows
	k on RS rows, p on WS rows
	A
	B

Mock Tartan

Abbreviation:
k1three – knit 1 st by wrapping the yarn round the needle three times.

Multiple of 8 sts plus 6. Two colours A and B.
Row 1 (RS) Using A, knit.
Row 2 Using A, knit.
Row 3 Using B, k1, sl 1 wyib, k2, sl 1 wyib, * k4, sl 1 wyib, k2, sl 1 wyib; rep from * to last st, k1.
Row 4 Using B, p1, sl 1 wyif, p2, sl 1 wyif, * p4, sl 1 wyif, p2, sl 1 wyif; rep from * to last st, p1.
Row 5 Using A, knit.
Row 6 Using A, k1, k1three, k2, k1three, * k4, k1three, k2, k1three; rep from * to last st, k1.
Row 7 Using B, k1, sl 1 wyib dropping extra loops from needle, k2, sl 1 wyib dropping extra loops, * k4, sl 1 wyib dropping extra loops, k2, sl 1 wyib dropping extra loops; rep from * to the last st, k1.
Row 8 Using B, as row 4.
Row 9 Using B, as row 3.
Row 10 Using B, as row 4.
Row 11 Using B, as row 3.
Row 12 Using B, as row 4.
Repeat these 12 rows.

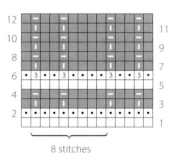

8 stitches

KEY

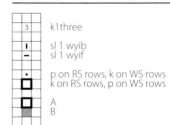

3	k1three
	sl 1 wyib
	sl 1 wyif
	p on RS rows, k on WS rows
	k on RS rows, p on WS rows
	A
	B

SLIP STITCH COLOUR PATTERNS

Easy Gingham

Multiple of 4 sts plus 2. Three colours A (medium), B (light) and C (dark).
Foundation Row Using A, purl.
Row 1 (RS) Using B, k1, sl 1 wyib, * k2, sl 2 wyib; rep from * to last 4 sts, k2, sl 1 wyib, k1.
Row 2 Using B, p1, sl 1 wyif, * p2, sl 2 wyif; rep from * to last 4 sts, p2, sl 1 wyif, p1.
Row 3 Using A, knit.
Row 4 Using C, p2, * sl 2 wyif, p2; rep from * to end.
Row 5 Using C, k2, * sl 2 wyib, k2; rep from * to end.
Row 6 Using A, purl.
Repeat these 6 rows.

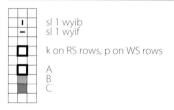

4 stitches

KEY

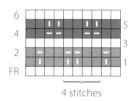

I	sl 1 wyib
—	sl 1 wyif
▢	k on RS rows, p on WS rows
▢	A
	B
	C

Slipped Stitch Fair Isle

Abbreviation:
dip st – insert RH needle from front to back through st 2 rows below next st on LH needle, yarn round needle and draw through a loop, place loop on to LH needle, then k2tog tbl the new loop and next st on LH needle.

Multiple of 4 sts plus 1. Three colours A, B and C.
Foundation Row 1 Using A, purl.
Row 1 (RS) Using C, k1, * sl 1 wyif, k1; rep from * to end.
Row 2 Using C, p2, * sl 1 wyib, p1; rep from * to last st, p1.
Row 3 Using A, knit.
Row 4 Using A, p2, * p1 wrapping yarn twice around needle, p3; rep from * to last 3 sts, p1 wrapping yarn twice around needle, p2.
Row 5 Using B, k2, * sl 1 wyib dropping extra loop from needle, k1, dip st, k1; rep from * to last 3 sts, sl 1 wyib dropping extra loop from needle, k2.

Row 6 Using B, p2, * sl 1 wyif, p3; rep from * to last 3 sts, sl 1 wyif, p2.
Row 7 Using B, knit.
Row 8 Using B, as row 4.
Row 9 Using A, as row 5.
Row 10 Using A, as row 6.
Row 11 Using A, knit.
Row 12 Using A, purl.
Row 13 Using C, as row 1.
Row 14 Using C, as row 2.
Row 15 Using B, knit.
Row 16 Using B, purl.
Row 17 Using A, k1, * sl 3 wyib, k1; rep from * to end.
Row 18 Using A, p2, * sl 1 wyif, p3; rep from * to last 3 sts, sl 1 wyif, p2.
Row 19 Using B, k4, * sl 1 wyib, k3; rep from * to last st, k1.
Row 20 Using B, purl.
Row 21 Using B, knit.
Row 22 Using B, purl.
Repeat these 22 rows.

KEY

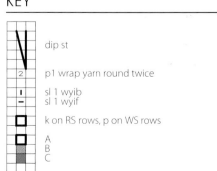

╲╱	dip st
2	p1 wrap yarn round twice
I	sl 1 wyib
—	sl 1 wyif
▢	k on RS rows, p on WS rows
▢	A
	B
	C

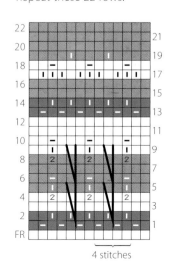

4 stitches

COLOUR STITCHES

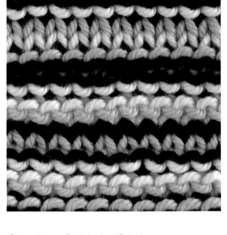

Daisy Stitch

Abbreviation:

daisy st – purl next 3 sts together without slipping them off the needle, yo, then purl the same 3 sts together again, slip them off the needle.

Multiple of 4 sts plus 1. Three colours A, B and C.

Row 1 (RS) Using A, knit.
Row 2 Using A, k1, * daisy st, k1; rep from * to end.
Row 3 Using B, knit.
Row 4 Using B, k1, p1, k1, * daisy st; k1; rep from * to last 2 sts, p1, k1.
Row 5 Using C, knit.
Row 6 Using C, as row 2.
Row 7 Using A, knit.
Row 8 Using A, as row 4.
Row 9 Using B, knit.
Row 10 Using B, as row 2.
Row 11 Using C, knit.
Row 12 Using C, as row 4.
Repeat these 12 rows.

Afghan Stitch

Multiple of 12 sts plus 3 (stitch count varies). Three colours A, B and C.

Row 1 Using A, k1, ssk, * k9, sl2tog-k1-psso; rep from * to last 12 sts, k9, k2tog, k1. 12 sts.
Row 2 Using A, k1, * p1, k4, (k1, yo, k1) into next st, k4; rep from * to last 2 sts, p1, k1. 15 sts.
Row 3 Using B, as row 1.
Row 4 Using B, as row 2.
Row 5 Using C, as row 1.
Row 6 Using C, as row 2.
Repeat these 6 rows.

Garter Stitch Stripes

Any number of sts. Three colours A, B and C.

Row 1 (RS) Using A, knit.
Row 2 Using B, knit.
Row 3 Using C, knit.
Row 4 Using A, knit.
Row 5 Using B, knit.
Row 6 Using C, knit.
Row 7 Using A, knit.
Row 8 Using B, purl.
Repeat these 8 rows, keeping colours in sequence and changing colour for each row.

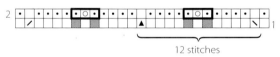

2 1

12 stitches

KEY

• ○ •	(k1, yo, k1) into next st
/	k2tog
\	ssk
▲	sl2tog-k1-psso
•	p on RS rows, k on WS rows
□	k on RS rows, p on WS rows
	no stitch

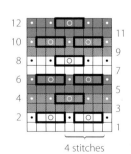

12 ... 11
10 ... 9
8 ... 7
6 ... 5
4 ... 3
2 ... 1

4 stitches

KEY

○	daisy st
•	p on RS rows, k on WS rows
□	k on RS rows, p on WS rows
	A B C

COLOUR STITCHES

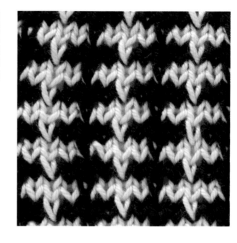

Cluster Stitch

Abbreviation:
cluster 3 sts – purl next 3 sts, slip these three sts on to a cable needle, wind yarn B 6 times clockwise around these 3 sts under the cable needle, slip sts back onto RH needle.

Multiple of 6 sts plus 5. Two colours A and B.
Row 1 (RS) Using A, knit.
Row 2 Using A, purl.
Row 3 Using A, knit.
Row 4 Using A, purl.
Row 5 Using B, knit.
Row 6 Using B, k4, * cluster 3 sts, k3; rep from * to last st, k1.
Row 7 Using A, knit.
Row 8 Using A, purl.
Row 9 Using A, knit.
Row 10 Using A, purl.
Row 11 Using B, knit.
Row 12 Using B, k1, * cluster 3 sts, k3; rep from * to last 4 sts, cluster 3 sts, k1.
Repeat these 12 rows.

Tea Cosy Stitch

Multiple of 16 sts plus 10. Two colours A and B.
Foundation Row 1 (RS) K1B, k8A, * carry B across back of A sts pulling up sts tightly then k8B, carry A across back of B sts pulling up sts tightly then k8A; rep from * to last st, carry B across back of A sts pulling up sts tightly then k1B.
Row 1 (WS) K9A, * carry B across front of A sts pulling up sts tightly then k8B, carry A across front of B sts pulling up sts tightly then k8A; rep from * to last st, carry B across front of A sts pulling up sts tightly then k1B.
Row 2 K9A, * carry B across back of A sts pulling up sts tightly then k8B, carry A across back of B sts pulling up sts tightly then k8A; rep from * to last st, carry B across back of A sts pulling up sts tightly then k1B.
Repeat these 2 rows.

Star Tweed

Abbreviation:
dip st - insert RH needle from front to back through st 2 rows below next st on LH needle (this will be the last row of the same colour below), yarn round needle and draw through a loop, place loop on to LH needle, then k2tog tbl the new loop and next st on LH needle.

Multiple of 4 sts plus 3. Two colours A and B.
Foundation Row 1 (WS) Using B, purl.
Foundation Row 2 Using A, knit.
Foundation Row 3 Using A, purl.
Row 1 (RS) Using B, * k3, dip st; rep from * to last 3 sts, k3.
Row 2 Using B, purl.
Row 3 Using A, k1, * dip st, k3; rep from * to last 2 sts, dip st, k1.
Row 4 Using A, purl.
Repeat these 4 rows.

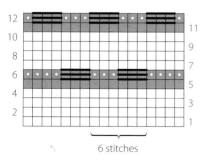

6 stitches

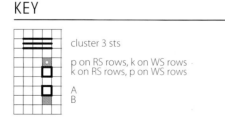

KEY

cluster 3 sts

p on RS rows, k on WS rows
k on RS rows, p on WS rows

A
B

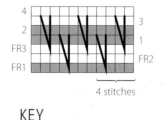

4 stitches

KEY

dip stitch

k on RS rows, p on WS rows

A
B

COLOUR STITCHES

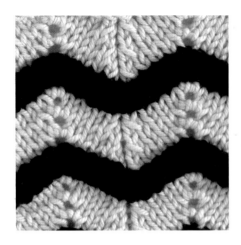

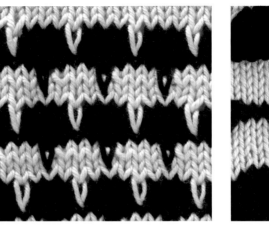

Embossed Stripes

Multiple of 11 sts plus 2. Two colours A and B.

Row 1 (RS) Using A, k1, * k2tog, k3, (k1, p1, k1) into next st, k3, ssk; rep from * to last st, k1.
Row 2 Using A, purl.
Row 3 Using A, as row 1.
Row 4 Using A, purl.
Row 5 Using A, as row 1.
Row 6 Using B, purl.
Row 7 Using B, purl.
Row 8 Using B, knit.
Row 9 Using B, purl.
Row 10 Using A, purl.
Repeat these 10 rows.

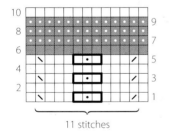

11 stitches

KEY

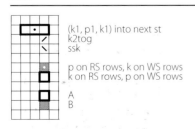

(k1, p1, k1) into next st
k2tog
ssk

p on RS rows, k on WS rows
k on RS rows, p on WS rows

A
B

Dip Stitch Check

Abbreviations:
dip st – insert RH needle from front to back through st 3 rows below next st on LH needle (this is into the first row of other colour), yarn round needle and draw through a loop loosely, place loop on to LH needle, then k2tog tbl new loop and next st on LH needle.

Multiple of 4 sts plus 3. Two colours A and B.
Foundation Row 1 Using A, knit.
Foundation Row 2 Using A, purl.
Row 1 (RS) Using A, knit.
Row 2 Using A, purl.
Row 3 Using B, k3, * dip st, k3; rep from * to end.
Row 4 Using B, purl.
Row 5 Using B, knit.
Row 6 Using B, purl.
Row 7 Using A, k1, * dip st, k3: rep from * to last 2 sts, dip st, k1.
Row 8 Using A, purl
Repeat these 8 rows.

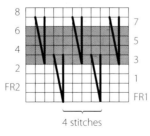

4 stitches

Short Row Bubbles

Multiple of 12 sts plus 4. Two colours A and B.
Row 1 (RS) Using A, knit.
Row 2 Using A, purl.
Using A, rep rows 1 and 2 twice more.
Row 7 Using B, knit.
Row 8 Using B, k12, * turn, p8, turn, k7, turn, p6, turn, k5, turn, p4, turn, k18; rep from * to last 4 sts, turn, p8, turn, k7, turn, p6, turn, k5, turn, p4, turn, k10.
Row 9 Using A, knit.
Row 10 Using A, purl.
Using A, rep rows 9 and 10 twice more.
Row 15 Using B, knit.
Row 16 Using B, k6, turn, p6, turn, k5, turn, p5, turn, k4, turn, p4, turn, * k18, turn, p8, turn, k7, turn, p6, turn, k5, turn, p4, turn; rep from * to last 16 sts, k16, turn, p6, turn, k6, turn, p5, turn, k5, turn, p4, turn, k4.
Repeat these 16 rows.

KEY

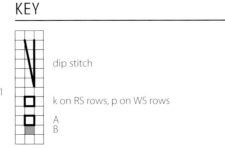

dip stitch

k on RS rows, p on WS rows

A
B

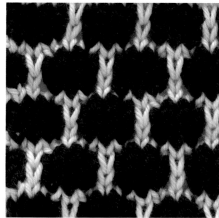

Blister Stitch

Abbreviation:

dropped dip st – insert RH needle from front to back through st 4 rows below next st on LH needle (this is into the last row of the same colour stripe below), drop next st off LH needle and unravel 4 rows down to held st, place this held st and 4 loose strands on to LH needle, then knit it, catching the 4 loose strands in the st.

Multiple of 4 sts plus 1. Two colours A and B.
Foundation Row 1 Using A, knit.
Foundation Row 2 Using A, purl.
Row 1 (RS) Using B, knit.
Row 2 Using B, purl.

Row 3 Using B, knit.
Row 4 Using B, purl.
Row 5 Using A, k2, * dropped dip st, k3; rep from * to last 3 sts, dropped dip st, k2.
Row 6 Using A, purl.
Row 7 Using B, knit.
Row 8 Using B, purl.
Row 9 Using B, knit.
Row 10 Using B, purl.
Row 11 Using A, k4, * dropped dip st, k3; rep from * to last st, k1.
Row 12 Using A, purl.
Repeat these 12 rows.

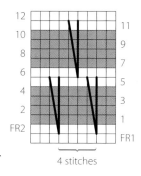

4 stitches

Shell Pattern

Abbreviations:

dropped dip st – insert RH needle from front to back through st 4 rows below next st on LH needle (this is into the last row of the 2nd stripe down), drop next st off LH needle and unravel 4 rows down to held st, place this held st and 4 loose strands on to LH needle, then knit it, catching the 4 loose strands in the st.
RT – (right twist) take RH needle in front of first st on LH needle and knit 2nd st, then knit first st, slip both sts off needle.
LT – (left twist) take RH needle behind first st on LH needle and knit 2nd st, then knit first st, slip both sts off needle.

Multiple of 6 sts plus 3. Three colours A, B and C.
Foundation Row 1 (WS) Using A, purl.

Foundation Row 2 Using B, knit.
Foundation Row 3 Using B, purl.
Foundation Row 4 Using B, k2, * LT, k1, RT, k1; rep from * to last st, k1.
Foundation Row 5 Using B, purl.
Row 1 (RS) Using C, k4, * dropped dip st, k5; rep from * to last 5 sts, dropped dip st, k4.
Row 2 Using C, purl.
Row 3 Using C, k2, * RT, k1, LT, k1; rep from * to last st, k1.
Row 4 Using C, purl.
Row 5 Using A, k1, * dropped dip st, k5; rep from * to last 2 sts, dropped dip st, k1.
Row 6 Using A, purl.
Row 7 Using A, k2, * LT, k1, RT, k1; rep from * to last st, k1.
Row 8 Using A, purl.
Repeat these 8 rows, using colours in sequence and changing colour after rows 4 and 8.

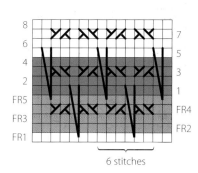

6 stitches

KEY

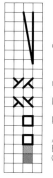

dropped dip st

right twist

left twist

k on RS rows, p on WS rows

A
B
C

PROJECTS

PATCHWORK CUSHION

This cushion is an example of the many exciting ways you can use the stitches in this book. These are texture stitches but if you prefer colour to texture, make squares using stitches from the Slip Stitch Colour Patterns and Colour Stitches sections (see pages 87–95). Choose yarns in colours to co-ordinate with your other furnishings. Use the cushion diagram as a layout template.

MEASUREMENTS
approximately 16in (40.5cm) square

GATHER TOGETHER...
Materials
1 x 1¾oz/50g ball of worsted (DK) weight cotton yarn (93yd/85m per ball) in colour
A pale grey
1 x 1¾oz/50g ball of worsted (DK) weight wool/cotton mix yarn (123yd/113m per ball) each in colours
B light blue violet
C pale lilac
D light pink
2 x 1¾oz/50g balls of worsted (DK) weight cotton yarn (92yd/84m per ball) in colour
E bright green
Backing fabric
16in (40.5cm) square cushion pad

Needles
1 pair of size 6 (4mm) needles

GAUGE
20 sts and 28 rows to 4in (10cm) measured over stockinette (stocking) stitch on size 6 (4mm) needles using **A**

Knit Your Cushion...
Square 1
Using size 6 (4mm/UK8) needles and **D**, cast on 27 sts and work 36 rows in Bobble Circle Pattern (see page 25).
Bind off in patt.

Square 2
Using size 6 (4mm) needles and **E**, cast on 30 sts and work 36 rows in Bramble Stitch (see page 23).
Bind off in patt.

Square 3
This is made up of four smaller squares.
Square 3A
Using size 6 (4mm) needles and **A**, cast on 15 sts and work 20 rows of Medallion Bobble Cable (see page 33).
Bind off in patt.
Square 3b
Using size 6 (4mm) needles and **B**, cast on 15 sts and work 20 rows in Moss Stitch (see page 10).
Bind off in patt.
Square 3c
Using size 6 (4mm) needles and **D**, cast on 13 sts and work 20 rows in Boxed Bobble (see page 24).
Bind off in patt.

Square 3d
Using size 6 (4mm) needles and **E**, cast on 18 sts and work 20 rows in Five Rib Braid (see page 34).
Bind off in patt.

Square 4
This is made up of four smaller squares.
Square 4a
Using size 6 (4mm) needles and **E**, cast on 16 sts and work 20 rows in Nosegay Pattern (see page 39).
Bind off in patt.
Square 4b
Using size 6 (4mm) needles and **B**, cast on 18 sts and work 20 rows in Two Stitch Check (see page 11).
Bind off in patt.
Square 4c
Using size 6 (4mm) needles and **C**, cast on 15 sts and work 20 rows in Mistake Rib (see page 28).
Bind off in patt.
Square 4d
Using size 6 (4mm) needles and **A**, cast on 21 sts and work 20 rows in Heart Cable (see page 39).
Bind off in patt.

Square 5
Using size 6 (4mm) needles and **C**, cast on 26 sts and work 36 rows in Stepped Diamonds pattern (see page 14).
Bind off in patt.

Square 6
Using size 6 (4mm) needles and **A**, cast on 31 sts and work 36 rows in Double Moss Stitch and Rib Check (see page 10).
Bind off in patt.

Square 7
Using size 6 (4mm) needles and **A**, cast on 29 sts and work 36 rows in Basketweave (see page 11).
Bind off in patt.

Square 8
Using size 6 (4mm) needles and **D**, cast on 30 sts and work 36 rows in Mock Cable (see page 14).
Bind off in patt.

Square 9
Using size 6 (4mm) needles and **E**, cast on 29 sts and work 36 rows in Heart Squares (see page 15).
Bind off in patt.

To Finish...
Block the large squares to about 5½in (14cm) square and the smaller ones to about 3in (7.5cm). These measures are a guide only; some of the smaller squares are slightly longer or narrower. The squares are sewn together using **E** with the seam on the outside; use a small neat running stitch.

Square 3
With WS together, sew 3A to 3C, and 3B to 3D. Sew the two strips together.

Square 4
With WS together, sew 4A to 4C, and 4B to 4D. Sew the two strips together.
Sew squares 1, 4 and 7 together, 2, 5 and 8 together, and then 3, 6 and 9 together.

Sew the three strips together. Block the whole piece to about 16in (40.5cm) square. Cut a piece of backing fabric to 17¼in (43.5cm) square. Neaten the edges and press a seam allowance of ⅝in (1.5cm) to the wrong side on all edges. With WS facing, place the front and back together and sew around three sides using a small neat running stitch. Insert the cushion pad and sew the remaining side closed.

1		2		3a	3b
1		2		3c	3d
4a	4b	5		6	
4c	4d	5		6	
7		8		9	

PLACE MAT AND COASTER

This place mat is made up of panels of stitches twisted symmetrically to the left and right forming heart-shaped outlines in the stockinette (stocking) stitch (see page 131). The handy pocket at the side is perfect for holding cutlery. A single panel is used on the seed (moss) stitch coaster.

MEASUREMENTS
Place mat measures 13in (33cm) wide by
10in (25.5cm) side
Coaster measures 4in (10cm) square

GATHER TOGETHER...
materials
3 x 1¾oz/50g balls of worsted (DK) weight
cotton yarn (92yd/84m per ball)
in bright green

needles
1 pair of size 6 (4mm) needles
Spare needle

GAUGE
22 sts and 29 rows to 4in (10cm)
measured over stockinette (stocking) stitch
on size 6 (4mm) needles

Knit Your Place Mat...
Pocket lining
Using size 6 (4mm) needles cast on
12 sts.
Row 1 P1, k3, RT, LT, k3, p1.
Row 2 P to end.
Row 3 P1, LT, RT, k2, LT, RT, p1.
Row 4 P1, k1, p8, k1, p1.
Row 5 P1, k1, RT, k4, LT, k1, p1.
Row 6 As row 4.
Row 7 P1, RT, k6, LT, p1.
Row 8 P to end.
Rep these 8 rows twice more, then rows 1 and
2 again.
Leave these 12 sts on a spare needle.

Place Mat
Using 6 (4mm) needles cast on 63 sts.
Row 1 P1, * k1, p1; rep from * to end.
This row forms seed (moss) st. Rep this row
twice more.
Inc row Seed (moss) st 7 sts, M1 knitwise,
(seed (moss) st 12 sts, M1 knitwise) 4 times,
seed (moss) st to end. 68 sts.
Start patt.
Row 1 P1, k1, p1, * k3, RT, LT, k3, p1, k1, p1; rep
from * to end.
Row 2 P1, k1, * p12, k1; rep from * to
last st, p1.
Row 3 P1, k1, p1, * LT, RT, k2, LT, RT, p1, k1, p1;
rep from * to end.
Row 4 (P1, k1) twice, * p8, (k1, p1) twice, k1;
rep from * to last 12 sts, p8, (k1, p1) twice.
Row 5 (P1, k1) twice, * RT, k4, LT, (k1, p1) twice,
k1; rep from * to last 12 sts, RT, k4, LT,
(k1, p1) twice.
Row 6 As row 4.
Row 7 P1, k1, p1, * RT, k6, LT, p1, k1, p1; rep
from * to end.
Row 8 As row 2.
Rep these 8 rows twice more, then rows 1 to
5 again.
Pocket border
Next row (WS) Patt to last 17 sts, (k1, p1)
twice, k1, p2tog, (k1, p1) 5 times.

Next row (P1, k1) 7 times, p1, patt to end.
Next row Patt to last 15 sts, (p1, k1)
7 times, p1.
Next row (P1, k1) 7 times, p1, patt to end.
Next row Patt to last 13 sts, cast off 11 sts in
patt, patt to end.
Join in pocket lining
Next row P1, k1, patt across 12 sts of pocket
lining, patt to end.
Cont in patt until piece measures approx 10in
(25cm) from beg, ending with row 5.
Dec row (P1, k1) twice, p2tog, * (k1, p1) 5
times, k1, p2tog; rep from * 4 times, (k1, p1)
5 times.
Seed (moss) st 3 rows.
Bind off in patt.

Knit Your Coaster...
Using size 6 (4mm) needles cast on 19 sts and
work 3 rows in seed (moss) st as given for mat.
Inc row Seed (moss) st 9 sts, M1 knitwise, seed
(moss) st to end. 20 sts.
Row 1 (P1, k1) twice, p1, k3, RT, LT, k3, (p1, k1)
twice, p1.
Row 2 (P1, k1) twice, p12, (k1, p1) twice.
Row 3 (P1, k1) twice, p1, LT, RT, k2, RT, LT,
(p1, k1) twice, p1.
Row 4 (P1, k1) 3 times, p8, (k1, p1) 3 times.
Row 5 (P1, k1) 3 times, RT, k4, LT, (k1, p1)
3 times.
Row 6 As row 4.
Row 7 (P1, k1) twice, p1, RT, k6, LT, (p1, k1)
twice, p1.
Row 8 (P1, k1) twice, p12, (k1, p1) twice.
Rep these 8 rows once more, then rows 1 to
5 again.
Dec row (P1, k1) 3 times, p2tog, (k1, p1)
6 times.
Seed (moss) st 3 rows.
Bind off in patt.

To Finish...
Block pieces to measurements. Sew pocket
lining to mat.

CABLE THROW

Each cable panel is knitted separately so this Throw is quick and easy to knit. The cable designs used for each panel are all included in the Stitch Library (see pages 32–45). You will also find additional cable patterns to choose from but make sure you choose a mix of large and small cables. The throw can be knitted in stripes as shown or all in one colour.

MEASUREMENTS
Throw measures approximately
46in (117cm) wide by 50in (127cm) long

GATHER TOGETHER...
materials
3 x 3½oz/100g hanks of chunky tweed-effect wool yarn (142yd/130m per hank)
in colours
A oatmeal
B blue green
C moss green
2 x 3½oz/100g hanks in colour
D grey
To make the throw in one colour you will need 11 hanks

needles
1 pair of size 10½ (7mm) needles
Cable needle

GAUGE
12 sts and 17 rows to 4in (10cm) measured over stockinette (stocking) stitch on size 10½ (7mm) needles

Basic Cable Panel
Using size 10½ (7mm) needles cast on number of stitches required for cable pattern plus 3 sts of rev st st and 3 sts of st st each side (cable pattern sts plus 12 sts).
Knit 3 rows.
Row 1 (RS) K3, p3, work first row of cable pattern, p3, k3.
Row 2 P3, k3, work 2nd row of cable pattern, k3, p3.
Cont in patt as set until cable panel measures 50in (127cm) from beg, ending with a RS row.
Knit 3 rows.
Bind off.

Celtic cable, panel 3

Triple twist cable, panel 5

Use these instructions to work the following cable panels.
Panel 1
Ripple and Rock (see page 36) using **C**.
Panel 2
Oxo Cable (see page 33) using **B**.
Panel 3
Celtic Cable (see page 34) using **A**.
Panel 4
Four Stitch Wave Cable (see page 32) using **D**.
Panel 5
Triple Twist Cable (see page 35) using **B**.
Panel 6
Six Stitch Cable – crosses every eighth row (see page 32) using **C**.
Panel 7
Hollow Oak (see page 35) using **D**.
Panel 8
Braid Cable (see page 36) using **A**.

To Finish...
Work as many panels as required. Block the pieces to length measurement. Lay the pieces out side by side and sew together.

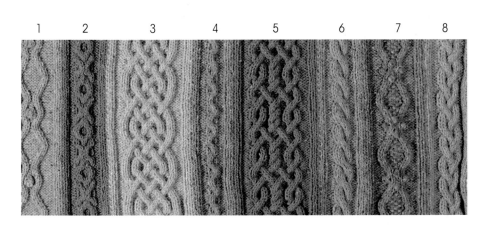

| 1 | 2 | 3 | 4 | 5 | 6 | 7 | 8 |

CROSSOVER CABLES

Two panels of cables make up this traditional poncho, which is worked in a heavy yarn. There is no shaping; you just cast on and work a thick centre cable with a smaller cable on each side. The cable panel uses C6F, C6B, Cr4L, and Cr4R (see page 138) to cross the stitches; it is a simple 18-row pattern that you will soon learn.

STITCH FOCUS

This poncho is made from two identical rectangles measuring 33in (84cm) long and 21in (54cm) wide. Sewn together, they form the poncho. Use this idea to work rectangles in your choice of stitches. Use different cables, such as the Heart Cable (see page 42) or a cable fabric, such as the Open Cables (see page 47). Experiment with colour and make the Two-Colour Cable (see page 43), or move away from cables altogether and try panels of textured stitches, such as Large Leaf Pattern (see page 27) or Smocked Honeycomb (see page 24). Whatever stitches you choose, use big yarns with big personalities and this poncho will knit up in no time.

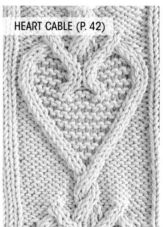
HEART CABLE (P. 42)

TWO-COLOUR CABLE (P. 43)

RE-STITCHED

The different panels of stitches in this design give you great scope for using your own choice of stitches to create a truly unique garment.

LARGE LEAF PATTERN (P. 27)

SMOCKED HONEYCOMB (P. 24)

Cables are historically associated with sturdy woollens such as bulky fishermen's sweaters. The cabled panels on this poncho work well used in this traditional way; they lend a pleasingly solid and chunky detail to the wonderfully warm garment.

This poncho has been sewn together to create a neck opening. If you prefer to wear it as a wrap, simply knit one piece as long as you want it.

MEASUREMENTS
74in (188cm) circumference at widest point and 21in (53.5cm) long on shoulder (when worn as a poncho with point at centre front and back)

GATHER TOGETHER...
materials
11 x 3½oz (100g) hanks of medium-weight (aran) multi-coloured wool yarn (150yd/138m per hank) in shades of green

needles and notions
1 pair of size 13 (9mm) needles
Cable needle
Stitch markers

GAUGE
10 sts and 12 rows to 4in (10cm) measured over st st using size 13 (9mm) needles and two strands of yarn together

KNIT. NOTE
Two yarns are used together to make a thicker yarn. Make sure that you work through both yarns for each stitch.

Special Abbreviations
C6F slip next 3 sts on to a cable needle at front of work, k3, then k3 from cable needle.

C6B slip next 3 sts on to a cable needle at back of work, k3, then k3 from cable needle.

Cr4L slip next 3 sts on to a cable needle at front of work, p1, then k3 from cable needle.

Cr4R slip next st on to a cable needle at back of work, k3, then p1 from cable needle.

KNITTING THE CABLE PATTERNS

Throughout the project pattern you will have to refer back to these instructions for knitting cable panels A, B and C:

Cable Panel A
(10 sts)
Row 1 RS P2, C6B, p2.
Row 2 K2, p6, k2.
Row 3 P2, k6, p2.
Row 4 As row 2.
Row 5 As row 3.
Row 6 K2, p6, k2.

Cable Panel B
(24 sts)
Row 1 RS P4, C6B, p4, C6F, p4.
Row 2 (K4, p6) twice, k4.
Row 3 P3, Cr4R, Cr4L, p2, Cr4R, Cr4L, p3.
Row 4 K3, (p3, k2) 3 times, p3, k3.
Row 5 P2, (Cr4R, p2, Cr4L) twice, p2.
Row 6 K2, p3, k4, p6, k4, p3, k2.
Row 7 P2, k3, p4, C6F, p4, k3, p2.

Row 8 As row 6.
Row 9 P2, k3, p4, k6, p4, k3, p2.
Row 10 As row 6.
Row 11 As row 9.
Row 12 As row 6.
Row 13 As row 7.
Row 14 As row 6.
Row 15 P2, (Cr4L, p2, Cr4R) twice, p2.
Row 16 As row 4.
Row 17 P3, Cr4L, Cr4R, p2, Cr4L, Cr4R, p3.
Row 18 (K4, p6) twice, k4.

Cable Panel C
(10 sts)
Row 1 RS P2, C6F, p2.
Row 2 K2, p6, k2.
Row 3 P2, k6, p2.
Row 4 As row 2.
Row 5 As row 3.
Row 6 K2, p2, k2.

Knit Your Poncho...

Work two pieces the same.
Using size 13 (9mm) needles and two strands of yarn together, cast on 65 sts loosely.
Row 1 RS K1, *p1, k1; rep from * to end.
Row 2 P1, *k1, p1; rep from * to end.
Row 3 As row 2.
Inc Row (K1, p1) 7 times, M1, k1, (p1, k1) 6 times, M1, (p1, k1, p1, M1, k1, p1, k1, M1) twice, (p1, k1) 6 times, M1, (p1, k1) 7 times. 72 sts.
Foundation Row 1 (K1, p1) twice, k5, p2, k6, p2, k5, (p4, k6) twice, p4, k5, p2, k6, p2, k5, (p1, k1) twice.
Foundation Row 2 (P1, k1) twice, p5, k2, p6, k2, p5, (k4, p6) twice, k4, p5, k2, p6, k2, p5, (k1, p1) twice.
Beg moss (double moss) stitch edges and panels.
Row 1 (P1, k1) twice, k5, work 1st row of panel A, k5, work 1st row of panel B, k5, work 1st row of panel C, k5, (k1, p1) twice.
Row 2 (K1, p1) twice, p5, work 2nd row of panel C, p5, work 2nd row of panel B, p5, work 2nd row of panel A, p5, (p1, k1) twice.
Row 3 (K1, p1) twice, k5, work 3rd row of panel A, k5, work 3rd row of panel B, k5, work 3rd row of panel C, k5, (p1, k1) twice.
Row 4 (P1, k1) twice, p5, work 4th row of panel C, p5, work 4th row of panel B, p5, work 4th row of panel A, p5, (k1, p1) twice.

These 4 rows form moss (double moss) stitch borders and set cable panels A, B and C.**
Cont in patt as set, starting with 5th row of panels A, B and C, until 6 repeats of panel B have been worked, ending with row 18.
Next Row (P1, k1) twice, k5, work 1st row of panel A, k5, work 1st row of panel B, k5, work 1st row of panel C, k5, (k1, p1) twice.
Dec Row Patt 13 sts, p2tog, patt 11 sts, (k2tog, patt 2 sts, p2tog, patt 2 sts) twice, p2tog, patt 13 sts, p2tog, patt to end. 65 sts.
Work 3 rows in moss (double moss) stitch. Bind off loosely in patt.

To Finish...

Sew in all ends. Block each piece to measure 33in (84cm) long and 21in (54cm) wide.
The two pieces are joined together to form a poncho as follows: with RS of work facing, place a marker on the right-hand side edge of one piece 21in (54cm) up from cast-on edge. Sew the bound-off edge of the second piece along the side of first piece from cast-on to marker. With RS of work facing, place a marker on the right-hand side edge of the second piece 21in (54cm) up from cast-on edge. Sew the bound-off edge of the first piece along the side of second piece from cast-on to marker.

CASHMERE CHIC SET

This four-piece set of scarf, beret, gloves and corsage is worked in a luxurious wool and cashmere mix yarn in a deep, rich shade of red. Knit the whole set or pick out individual pieces to make up your own look. The scarf and beret are knitted in seed (moss) stitch using two strands of the yarn, producing a lush, richly textured fabric. The gloves and corsage need more precise shaping so are worked in one strand of yarn. The gloves have a pretty heart motif on the back of each hand, and the petals of the corsage are worked in garter stitch.

STITCH FOCUS

Ring the changes by using a different edging on the scarf and maybe using a contrasting colour or a textured yarn like mohair. For a scalloped edge, use Fir Tree Border (see page 80). Birch Leaf Edging (see page 80) or Lacy Leaf Edging (see page 81) are more open. A Seaweed Fringe (see page 82) will give a frothy, fun finish to the scarf.

FIR TREE BORDER (P. 80)

RE-STITCHED

Close-knit textured stitches will give you a warm winter set. Experiment with more open lace stitches for pretty garments that will still keep you cosy in milder spring and autumn weather.

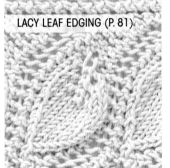
LACY LEAF EDGING (P. 81)

BIRCH LEAF EDGING (P. 80)

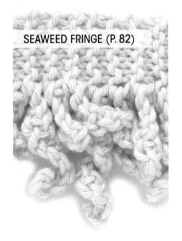
SEAWEED FRINGE (P. 82)

SCARF

The fancy ends of this scarf can be threaded through the keyhole to keep the scarf snug around your neck even on the windiest of days. It is worked in seed (moss) stitch using two strands of yarn together, so is very quick to knit. The large holes in the edgings are made with multiple yarnovers (yos) and then several stitches are worked into them (see page 137).

The lacy edging on the scarf provides an attractive flounce of detail.

MEASUREMENTS
5½in (14cm) wide by 40in (101.5cm) long

GATHER TOGETHER...
materials
3 x 1¾oz (50g) balls of light-weight (DK) wool/cashmere mix yarn (142yd/130m per ball) in claret red

needles
1 pair of size 10 (6mm) needles

GAUGE
16 sts and 26 rows to 4in (10cm) measured over seed (moss) stitch using size 10 (6mm) needles and two strands of yarn together

KNIT NOTE
Two strands are used together to make a thicker yarn. Make sure that you work through both strands for each stitch.

Knit Your Scarf...
Using size 10 (6mm) needles and two strands of yarn together, cast on 20 sts loosely.
Row 1 RS *K1, p1; rep from * to end.
Row 2 *P1, k1; rep from * to end.
These 2 rows form seed (moss) stitch and are repeated.
Cont in patt until scarf measures 4in (10cm), ending with a WS row.
Divide for keyhole:
Next Row Patt 10 sts, join in a new yarn (of two strands) and use this to patt to end.
Working both sides at the same time, work in patt until keyhole measures 3in (7.5cm), ending with a WS row.
Next Row Patt across all 20 sts (joining two sides into one again).
Cut off second yarn.
Cont in patt until scarf measures 32in (81.5cm), ending with a WS row.
Bind off loosely in patt.

Edging (make 2)
Using size 10 (6mm) needles and two strands of yarn together, cast on 13 sts loosely.
Foundation Row 1 K3, p10.
Foundation Row 2 K2, (yo) 4 times, k2tog, k6, turn.

Row 1 P7, (k1, p1) twice into 4 yo loop, p2.
Row 2 K16.
Row 3 K3, p13.
Row 4 K2, (yo) 5 times, k2tog, k9 and turn.
Row 5 P10, (k1, p1, k1, p1, k1) into 5 yo loop, p2.
Row 6 K20.
Row 7 K3, p17.
Row 8 Bind off 7 sts, k2 (including last st used in bind-off), (yo) 4 times, k2tog, k6 and turn.
These 8 rows form the edging and are repeated.
Cont in patt until edging fits across end of scarf, ending with row 7 of patt.
Bind off loosely.

To Finish...
Sew in all ends. Press according to instructions on ball band. Sew an edging onto each end of the scarf.

BERET

Using two strands of yarn together, the stylish beret is worked in seed (moss) stitch. The k1, p1 rib fits snugly around your head. After the rib, you increase stitches using M1 (see page 134), then shape the crown using p3tog and k3tog (see page 136) so that the seed (moss) stitch pattern isn't interrupted.

MEASUREMENTS
To fit head circumference 20 [22]in (51 [56]cm)

GATHER TOGETHER...
materials
2 x 1¾oz (50g) balls of light-weight (DK) wool/cashmere mix yarn (142yd/130m per ball) in claret red

needles
1 pair of size 8 (5mm) needles
1 pair of size 10 (6mm) needles

GAUGE
16 sts and 26 rows to 4in (10cm) measured over seed (moss) stitch using size 10 (6mm) needles and two strands of yarn together

Knit Your Beret...
Using size 8 (5mm) needles and two strands of yarn together, cast on 68 [76] sts.
Row 1 *K1, p1; rep from * to end.
This row forms the rib.
Work a further 4 rows in rib.
Inc Row Rib 4 [6], (rib 1 [2], M1, rib 2, M1) 20 [16] times, rib 4 [6]. 108 sts.
Change to size 10 (6mm) needles.
Row 1 RS *K1, p1; rep from * to end.
Row 2 *P1, k1; rep from * to end.
These 2 rows form seed (moss) stitch and are repeated. Work a further 20 rows in patt.

Shape Top
Row 23 K1, p1, k1, *p3tog, (k1, p1) 3 times, k3tog, (p1, k1) 3 times; rep from * to last 15 sts, p3tog, (k1, p1) 3 times, k3tog, p1, k1, p1. 84 sts.
Patt 7 rows.

Row 31 K1, p1, *k3tog, (p1, k1) twice, p3tog, (k1, p1) twice; rep from * to last 12 sts, k3tog, (p1, k1) twice, p3tog, k1, p1. 60 sts.
Patt 7 rows.
Row 39 K1, *p3tog, k1, p1, k3tog, p1, k1; rep from * to last 9 sts, p3tog, k1, p1, k3tog, p1. 36 sts.
Patt 3 rows.
Row 43 *K1, p1, k1, p3tog; rep from * to end. 24 sts.
Patt 1 row.
Row 45 *K3tog, p1; rep from * to end. 12 sts.
Purl 1 row.
Cut yarn and thread through rem sts. Pull up tight and fasten off.

To Finish...
Sew in all ends. Press according to instructions on ball band. Join back seam.

CORSAGE

Each of the six petals is knitted separately; they are then joined at the base to produce a large bloom. The petal is shaped by working three times into one st (see page 135) and decreased using ssk, k2tog and sl2tog-k1-psso (see page 136). The centre is filled with sequins and beads.

MEASUREMENTS
Flower is approx 5in (12.5cm) in diameter

GATHER TOGETHER...
materials
1 x 1¾oz (50g) balls of light-weight (DK) wool/cashmere mix yarn (142yd/130m per ball) in claret red
Sequins and small beads

needles and notions
1 pair of size 3 (3.25mm) needles
Brooch pin or safety pin

gauge
24 sts and 48 rows to 4in (10cm) measured over garter stitch (every row k) using size 3 (3.25mm) needles and one strand of yarn

Knit Your Corsage...
Petal (make 6)
Using size 3 (3.25mm) needles and single strand of yarn, cast on 3 sts and knit 1 row.
Row 1 RS K1, (k into front, back and front) into next st, k1. 5 sts.
Rows 2, 4, 6 Knit.
Row 3 K2, (k into front, back and front) into next st, k2. 7 sts.
Row 5 K3, (k into front, back and front) into next st, k3. 9 sts.
Row 7 K4, (k into front, back and front) into next st, k4. 11 sts.
Knit 5 rows.
Row 13 K1, ssk, k5, k2tog, k1. 9 sts.
Knit 5 rows.
Row 19 K1, ssk, k3, k2tog, k1. 7 sts.
Knit 3 rows.

Row 23 K1, ssk, k1, k2tog, k1. 5 sts.
Knit 3 rows.
Row 27 K1, sl2tog-k1-psso, k1. 3 sts.
Knit 1 row.
Row 29 Sl2tog-k1-psso. 1 st.
Cut yarn and thread through rem st.

To Finish...
Sew in all ends. Fold each petal in half (with RS together) at the base and sew the side edges together for ½in (1.5cm). Place the petals side by side and run a gathering thread through each to join. Pull the thread tight and repeat through all petals again to form a circle. Pull the thread tight so the flower becomes dish-shaped. Secure the thread. Fill the centre with sequins and beads, sewing the beads onto the top of the sequins. Sew a brooch pin or safety pin on to the back.

GLOVES

To make the gloves fit perfectly, use one strand of yarn throughout and stockinette stitch. There is a k1, p1 rib cuff for a snug fit. The thumb gusset is shaped out from the hand using M1 (see page 134) and the fingers are shaped at the top using k2tog (see page 136).

MEASUREMENTS
To fit sizes S [M:L]; width around palm is 7 [8:8¾]in (18 [20.5:22]cm) and 7 [7½:8]in (18 [19:20.5]cm) long from wrist

GATHER TOGETHER...
materials
2 [2:2] x 1¾oz (50g) balls of light-weight (DK) wool/cashmere mix yarn (142yd/130m per ball) in claret red

needles
1 pair of size 3 (3.25mm) needles
1 pair of size 6 (4mm) needles

gauge
22 sts and 30 rows to 4in (10cm) measured over st st (1 row k, 1 row p) using size 6 (4mm) needles and one strand of yarn

Heart Motif Panel
(13 sts)
Row 1 RS K6, p1, k6.
Row 2 P5, k1, p1, k1, p5.
Row 3 K4, p1, (k1, p1) twice, k4.
Row 4 P3, k1, (p1, k1) 3 times, p3.
Row 5 K2, p1, (k1, p1) 4 times, k2.
Row 6 P1, (k1, p1) 6 times.
Row 7 As row 6.
Row 8 As row 6.
Row 9 As row 6.
Row 10 As row 6.
Row 11 As row 6.
Row 12 As row 6.
Row 13 K2, p1, k1, p1, k3, p1, k1, p1, k2.
Row 14 P3, k1, p5, k1, p3.
These 14 rows form the heart motif panel.

Knit Your Right Glove...
Using size 3 (3.25mm) needles and one strand of yarn, cast on 40 [44:48] sts loosely.
Row 1 *K1, p1; rep from * to end.
Rep this row until rib measures 2½in (6cm).
Change to size 6 (4mm) needles and work 2 rows in st st (1 row k, 1 row p), starting with a k row.**

Shape Thumb Gusset
Next Row K20 [22:24], M1, k2, M1, k18 [20:22]. 42 [46:50] sts.
Work 3 rows in st st.
Next Row K20 [22:24], M1, k4, M1, k18 [20:22]. 44 [48:52] sts.
Work 3 rows in st st.
Next Row K20 [22:24], M1, k6, M1, k18 [20:22]. 46 [50:54] sts.
Work 3 rows in st st.
Next Row K4 [5:6], work row 1 of heart motif panel, k3 [4:5], M1, k8, M1, k18 [20:22]. 48 [52:56] sts.

Next Row P31 [34:37], work row 2 of heart motif panel, p4 [5:6].
Next Row K4 [5:6], work row 3 of heart motif panel, k31 [34:37].
Next Row P31 [34:37] work row 4 of heart motif panel, p4 [5:6].
Next Row K4 [5:6], work row 5 of heart motif panel, k3 [4:5], M1, k10, M1, k18 [20:22]. 50 [54:58] sts.
Next Row P33 [36:39], work row 6 of heart motif panel, p4 [5:6].

Thumb
Next Row K4 [5:6], work row 7 of heart motif panel, k15 [16:17], and turn.
Next Row Cast on 2 sts (using cable cast-on – see page 128), p14 (including 2 sts just cast on), turn and cast on 2 sts.
***Work 2½ [2¾:3]in (6 [7:7.5]cm) on these 16 sts only for thumb, ending with a p row. Measure the knitting next to your thumb, placing cast-on sts at base of your thumb. You may need to add or subtract rows here to fit your thumb length.
Next Row K1, (k2tog, k1) 5 times. 11 sts.
P 1 row.
Next Row K1, (k2tog) 5 times.
Cut yarn and thread through rem 6 sts. Pull up tight and fasten off. Join thumb seam.
With RS of work facing, using size 6 (4mm) needles, pick up and k 2 sts across base of thumb, k across 18 [20:22] unworked sts on left-hand needle. 40 [44:48] sts.
****Keeping heart motif panel correct (beg with row 8), cont in st st without shaping until work measures 1½ [1¾:2]in (4 [4.5:5]cm) from pick-up sts at base of thumb, ending with a p row. Try the glove on; it should reach the base of your fingers. You may need to add or subtract rows here to fit your hand length.

The cute heart-shaped motif is worked on the back of each hand in seed (moss) stitch to stand out well against the stockinette stitch.

After working the st st for each finger, try the glove on and measure the knitting against your fingers. Adjust the length as required.

First Finger

Next Row K25 [27:30] sts and turn.
Next Row Cast on 2 sts, p12 [12:14] (including 2 sts just cast on), turn and cast on 2 sts.
Work 2½in (6cm) on these 14 [14:16] sts only for first finger, ending with a p row.
Next Row K1, (k2tog, k1) 4 [4:5] times, k1 [1:0]. 10 [10:11] sts.
P 1 row.
Next Row K1, (k2tog) 4 [4:5] times, k1 [1:0]. Cut yarn and thread through rem 6 sts. Pull up tight and fasten off. Join finger seam.

Second Finger

With RS of work facing, using size 6 (4mm) needles pick up and k 2 sts across base of first finger, k5 [6:6] sts and turn.
Next Row Cast on 1 st, p13 [15:15] (including st just cast on), turn and cast on 1 st.
Work 1in (7cm) on these 14 [16:16] sts only for second finger, ending with a p row.
Next Row K1, (k2tog, k1) 4 [5:5] times, k1 [0:0]. 10 [11:11] sts.
P 1 row.
Next Row K1, (k2tog) 4 [5:5] times, k1 [0:0]. Cut yarn and thread through rem 6 sts. Pull up tight and fasten off. Join finger seam.

Third Finger

With RS of work facing, using size 6 (4mm) needles pick up and k 2 sts across base of second finger, k5 [6:6] sts and turn.
Next Row Cast on 1 st, p13 [15:15] (including st just cast on), turn and cast on 1 st.

Work 2½in (6cm) on these 14 [16:16] sts only for first finger, ending with a p row.
Next Row K1, (k2tog, k1) 4 [5:5] times, k1 [0:0]. 10 [11:11] sts.
P 1 row.
Next Row K1, (k2tog) 4 [5:5] times, k1 [0:0]. Cut yarn and thread through rem 6 sts. Pull up tight and fasten off. Join finger seam.

Fourth Finger

With RS of work facing, using size 6 (4mm) needles, pick up and k 4 sts across base of third finger, k across 5 [5:6] unworked sts to end.
Next Row P across all 14 [14:16] rem sts.
Work 2in (5cm) on these 14 [14:16] sts only for fourth finger, ending with a p row.
Next Row K1, (k2tog, k1) 4 [4:5] times, k1 [1:0]. 10 [10:11] sts.
P 1 row.
Next Row K1, (k2tog) 4 [4:5] times, k1 [1:0]. Cut yarn and thread through rem 6 sts. Pull up tight and fasten off.

Knit Your Left Glove...

Work as given for right glove to **.

Shape Thumb Gusset

Next Row K18 [20:22], M1, k2, M1, k20 [22:24]. 42 [46:50] sts.
Work 3 rows in st st.
Next Row K18 [20:22], M1, k4, M1, k20 [22:24]. 44 [48:52] sts.
Work 3 rows in st st.
Next Row K18 [20:22], M1, k6, M1, k20 [22:24]. 46 [50:54] sts.
Work 3 rows in st st.
Next Row K18 [20:22], M1, k8, M1, k3 [4:5], work row 1 of heart motif panel, k4 [5:6]. 48 [52:56] sts.

Next Row P4 [5:6], work row 2 of heart motif panel, p31 [34:37].
Next Row K31 [34:37], work row 3 of heart motif panel, k4 [5:6].
Next Row P4 [5:6], work row 4 of heart motif panel, p31 [34:37].
Next Row K18 [20:22], M1, k10, M1, k3 [4:5], work row 5 of heart motif panel, k4 [5:6]. 50 [54:58] sts.

Next Row P4 [5:6], work row 6 of heart motif panel, p33 [36:39].

Thumb

Next Row K30 [32:34] and turn.
Next Row Cast on 2 sts, p14 (including 2 sts just cast on), turn and cast on 2 sts.
Complete as given for thumb of right glove from ***.
With RS of work facing, using size 6 (4mm) needles, pick up and k 2 sts across base of thumb, k3 [4:5], work row 7 of heart motif panel, k4 [5:6] across unworked sts on left-hand needle. 40 [44:48] sts.
Work as given for right glove from ****.

To Finish...

Sew in all ends. Press pieces according to instructions on ball band. Join side seams.

FALLING LEAVES

This baguette-style bag has a delightfully neat, chic shape. It is made in a warm, cosy fabric produced from green tweed wool with slots of fiery colours worked in a contrasting stitch. The bag has been fulled, which produces a lovely dense texture. The contrasting colours are strong and yet subtle. This is a bag that is full of detail and interest while retaining an understated stylishness.

STITCH FOCUS

Create a simple bag by making two rectangles and sewing them together around three sides. For an easy finish, add ready-made handles. You can get a similar effect to this bag by using any of the slip stitch colour patterns on pages 85–91. Colour stitches such as the Mock Tartan (see page 90) and the Dip Stitch Check (see page 94) also work well. If you are going to full the bag, use a 100% wool yarn. Alternatively leave the bag unfulled and use a simple knit and purl stitch such as Basketweave (see page 11), or use stockinette (stocking) stitch and incorporate one of the Gansey patterns such as Humber Star (see page 21) as a central feature.

MOCK TARTAN (P. 90)

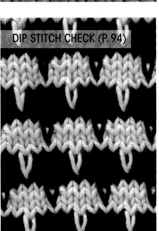
DIP STITCH CHECK (P. 94)

RE-STITCHED

A simple, compact bag shape is quick to knit and ideal for experimenting with combining different stitches.

BASKETWEAVE (P. 11)

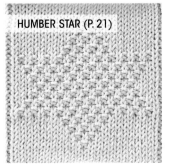
HUMBER STAR (P. 21)

The stitch pattern used for this bag is blind buttonhole stitch (full instructions for this are given below). This is a great way to introduce colour and texture without having to work with more than one yarn at a time. The bag is knitted on circular needles, transferring to flat knitting for the shaping at the top edges. The curved edge is made by binding off and decreasing stitches. The bag is closed with a zip, inserted after fulling.

MEASUREMENTS
Before fulling – 12½in (32cm) wide and 6½in (16.5cm) long from base to zip
After fulling – 11½in (29cm) wide and 6in (15cm) long

GATHER TOGETHER...
Materials
A 2 x 1¾oz (50g) balls of light-weight (DK) tweed wool (123yd/113m per ball) in green with orange and yellow flecks
B 6 x 8m skeins of tapestry wool in dark ginger, orange, light orange, dark yellow-orange, rust, light rust

Needles and notions
Size 6 (4mm) 24in (60cm)-long circular needles
1 pair of size 6 (4mm) needles
Stitch markers
Zip – measure length of opening after fulling

GAUGE
20 sts and 28 rows to 4in (10cm) measured over st st using size 6 (4mm) needles

KNIT NOTE

B is used to indicate the contrasting colours. Use one for each set of 4 patt rounds, choosing them randomly. When slipping stitches, carry the yarn loosely across the back of the work. Do not pull tight.

Special Abbreviations
sl 2(4) wyib slip 2 (4) sts purlwise with yarrn at back of work

Knit Your Bag...
Back and Front (worked in one piece)
Using size 6 (4mm) circular needles and **A**, cast on 128 sts.
Spread the stitches evenly around the needle, making sure the cast-on edge faces inward and is not twisted. Place a marker on the right-hand needle (this indicates the beginning of each round and is slipped on every round), bring the two needles together and purl the first st on the left-hand needle, pulling up the yarn to prevent a gap. Continue purling each cast-on st to reach the marker.
Purl 9 more rows.
Commence blind buttonhole st.
Round 1 Using **B, k2, sl 4 wyib, *k4, sl 4 wyib; rep from * to last 2 sts, k2.
Rep this round 3 times more.
Round 5 Using **A**, k2, p4, *k4, p4; rep from * to last 2 sts, k2.
Using **A**, p 3 rounds.
Round 9 Using **B**, sl 2 wyib, k4, *sl 4 wyib, k4; rep from * to last 2 sts, sl 2 wyib.
Rep this round 3 times more.
Round 13 Using **A**, p2, k4, *p4, k4; rep from * to last 2 sts, p2.
Using **A**, p 3 rounds.**
Rep from ** to ** twice more.

Shape Top
Next Round P24, bind off 16 sts, p48 (including last st used in binding off), bind off 16 sts, p24, remove marker, p24 and turn. From now on use the circular needle as you would straight needles – working backwards and forwards, turning at the end of each row. **Working on the first set of 48 sts, bind off 6 sts at beg of next 2 rows, and 5 sts at beg of foll 2 rows. Place markers at each end of last row.
Bind off 4 sts at beg of next 2 rows. 18 sts.
Dec 1 st at each end of every row to 8 sts, ending with a p row.
Bind off.
With RS of work facing, rejoin yarn to rem 48 sts and p to end, turn.
Work as given for first side from **.

Strap
Using size 6 (4mm) needles and **A**, cast on 10 sts.
Work 24in (61cm) in st st (1 row k, 1 row p), ending with a p row.
Bind off.

To Finish...
Sew in all ends. Lay bag flat, with beginning of cast-on edge at one side. Place a marker at the opposite fold for other side seam. Join base seam. To create the flat base, push the corners in and, on the WS, sew across the point 1in (2.5cm) from the tip. Join curved edges together from bound-off sts down to markers.

Fulling
Full a test sample of your knitting before attempting to full the finished bag; make sure you measure the sample before and after fulling to see how much it shrinks.

Turn the bag inside out. To full by hand, dissolve laundry soap or soap flakes into hot water (do not use detergent or washing powder). Knead the fabric without pulling or rubbing it together. Remove the fabric from the water frequently to check the fulling process after rinsing in cold water. If the fabric still moves apart easily, continue the fulling, making sure the temperature of the water is kept hot. When the fabric is dense and has a fuzzy appearance, rinse out the soap and dry flat. If you prefer to full in your washing machine, add the soap and bag together with towels to fill the machine and to provide friction. Run the shortest hot wash/cold rinse cycle but do not spin. Remove from the machine whenever possible to check the process.

To keep some of the depth of the blind buttonhole stitch, full the bag until the stitches just begin to mesh together. Keep pulling the strands of **B** away from the background fabric. Full the strap more so that the stitches disappear and the fabric becomes fuzzy. Keep pulling the edges out so they don't roll together. Dry as instructed, pushing a thin mould into the bag to give it a box shape.

Measure the handle cut to the desired length plus 2in (5cm) from overlaps (fulled fabric won't unravel once cut). My strap is 20in (51cm) finished length. Place one end on the side of the bag on the RS. Sew into place. Sew on the other end to match. Sew in the zip along the curved edges.

LACY LOVELY

This pretty, feminine bag is just the thing for a special occasion. It can be knitted in a cream cotton yarn to carry on a hot summer's day, or transformed into a glamourous bag for the evening, simply by changing the colour and shoulder strap. The beauty and delicacy of lace may not seem to lend itself to bags, which tend to get a lot of wear and tear. However, the introduction of a lining gives the bag sufficient robustness to make it usable, while also serving to make the intricacy and openness of the lace stitches stand out more. This bag is ideal if you are new to lace knitting; it isn't very big, so will take no time to knit.

STITCH FOCUS

This is a drawstring bag with a shaped base. You can make a simpler version by knitting a wide triangle and folding it in half, joining one side seam and the base, then working a row of simple eyelets and inserting a drawstring. Use any of the lace stitch patterns on pages 56–67. For a less open finish, consider using Gothic Window (see page 58) or Norwegian Fir (see page 60). Alternatively why not try using repeats of the Flower Panel (see page 70) between bands of stockinette (stocking) stitch? A drop stitch pattern such as Bluebell stitch (see page 74) would look equally pretty.

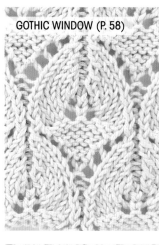

GOTHIC WINDOW (P. 58)

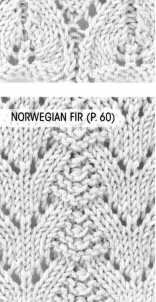

NORWEGIAN FIR (P. 60)

RE-STITCHED

Lace fabrics do not have to be white or cream. For a dramatic evening look, try making your bag in black, purple or red.

FLOWER PANEL (P. 70)

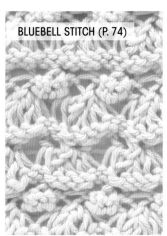

BLUEBELL STITCH (P. 74)

This bag is worked in an easy lace pattern with an eight-row repeat. The large holes are made by throwing three yarn overs (yo – see page 137) around the needle and then working five stitches into them. The smaller holes are worked into two yarn overs and one yarn over. The lace is worked only on the sides of the bag; stitches are picked up and then decreased to form a flat circular base.

MEASUREMENTS

Finished bag measures 20in (51cm) in circumference and 9in (23cm) in height

GATHER TOGETHER...

Materials

1 x 3½oz (100g) ball of fine-weight (4ply) cotton yarn (370yd/338m per ball) in cream

Needles and notions

1 pair of size 3 (3.25mm) needles
2 size 3 (3.25mm) double-pointed needles
Lining fabric 24in (61cm) x 10in (25.5cm)

Gauge

2 repeats of lace pattern (29 sts) measure 3½in (9cm) using size 3 (3.25mm) needles; 32 rows to 4in (10cm) measured over lace pattern

KNIT NOTE

The special binding-off technique used for this bag creates a picot edge – that is, the pointed tips around the top. This helps complete the delicate lacy look of the bag.

Knit Your Bag...

Using size 3 (3.25mm) needles, cast on 169 sts loosely and purl 1 row.

Row 1 RS K1, *ssk, k9, k2tog, k1; rep from * to end. 145 sts.

Row 2 P1, *p2tog, p7, ssp, p1; rep from * to end. 121 sts.

Row 3 K1, *ssk, k2, (yo) 3 times, k3, k2tog, k1; rep from * to end. 133 sts.

Row 4 P1, *p2tog, p2, (k1, p1, k1, p1, k1) into 3 yos, p1, ssp, p1; rep from * to end. 133 sts.

Row 5 K1, *ssk, k6, k2tog, k1; rep from * to end. 109 sts.

Row 6 P1, *p2tog, p6; rep from * to end. 97 sts.

Row 7 K1, *k2, yo, k1, (yo) twice, k1, (yo) twice, k1, yo, k3; rep from * to end. 169 sts.

Row 8 P1, *p2, p into yo, p1, (k1, p1) into 2 yos, p1, (k1, p1) into 2 yos, p1, p into yo, p3; rep from * to end. 169 sts.

These 8 rows form the lace pattern. Repeat these 8 rows 7 times more.

Knit 2 rows.

Picot Bind-Off Row Bind off 2 sts, *cast on 2 sts, bind off 5 sts; rep from * to end.

Sew in all ends. Using pins, stretch the bag out so it measures 20in (51cm) wide and 9in (23cm) high. Pin the bottom edge so that it is straight but leave the top edge in points. Gently steam, according to instructions on ball band. When the bag is dry, remove the pins.

Base

With RS of work facing and using size 3 (3.25mm) needles, pick up and knit 169 sts evenly around cast-on edge of bag.

Row 1 and every foll WS row Purl.

Row 2 K1, (ssk, k12) 12 times. 157 sts.

Row 4 K1, (ssk, k11) 12 times. 145 sts.

Row 6 K1, (ssk, K10) 12 times. 133 sts.

Row 8 K1, (ssk, k9) 12 times. 121 sts.

Cont to dec as set working 1 st less between each dec to 13 sts.

Cut yarn and thread through rem sts. Pull up tight and fasten off.

Drawstring/Strap

Using size 3 (3.25mm) double-pointed needles, cast on 5 sts.

Knit 1 row. Do not turn the work but slide the sts to the other end of the needle. Pull up the yarn and knit the sts again. Repeat until cord measures 42in (106.5cm). Bind off.

To Finish...

Press the base according to instructions on ball band.

Lining

Cut a piece of lining fabric 9¼in (23.5cm) long by 23½in (59.5cm) wide. Make a hem on each side by folding in ⅞in (1.5cm) and then folding this over again. Tack the hems down temporarily by using large running stitches in a contrasting thread. Press and sew around each edge neatly. Remove tacking stitches. Place the RS of the lining onto the WS of the bag. Slipstitch the bottom of the lining to the cast-on edge and the top to the row at the beg of the 7th pattern repeat, leaving one st on each edge of the side seam free. Join side seam of bag. Slipstitch the lining side seam closed. Thread the cord through the large holes in the 7th pattern repeat. Join the ends of the cord.

MAKING WAVES

You can create truly stunning effects with relatively simple techniques. The wave pattern featured here would be eye-catching if knitted in one plain yarn; the combination of two contrasting and vivid yarns, with different textures, mix together to create something truly unique. The soft waves in this scarf are created by an eight-row stitch pattern using two contrasting yarns. The wave of brightly coloured yarn is worked in garter stitch, while the green background is shaped by p2tog, p3tog (see page 136) and yo (see page 137). The colour switches are easy to handle; simply carry the yarn not in use up the side of the work.

STITCH FOCUS

Scarves are great ways to experiment with different stitches and are fun and quick to knit. There are many ways to make wave-like patterns in knitting. Why not try knitting a scarf using the Moss Stitch Chevron pattern (see page 14) in a single colour? Old Shale Pattern (see page 66) will give your scarf a beautiful and delicate air. And if you want to turn things on their head and have your waves going up and down instead of across the scarf, check out the Zigzag Eyelets (see page 72). You can even use the Woven Cables pattern (see page 46) if you like working with cables.

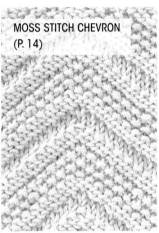
MOSS STITCH CHEVRON (P. 14)

OLD SHALE PATTERN (P. 66)

RE-STITCHED

In addition to changing the pattern, why not try using two different weights of yarn to add interest to your scarf?

ZIGZAG EYELETS (P. 72)

WOVEN CABLES (P. 46)

This scarf is made in relatively light-weight materials; the idea was to create a scarf that was more of a colourful accent than a practical and cosy item. If you like the wave pattern but also want to keep warm, simply make the scarf longer and in heavier yarns.

This scarf is perfect for when you want to add a dash of dramatic colour to an outfit.

MEASUREMENTS

42in (106cm) long by 5½in (14cm) wide

GATHER TOGETHER...
materials

A 1 x 1¾oz (50g) balls of light-weight (DK) wool yarn (131yd/120m per ball) in bright green

B 1 x 1¾oz (50g) balls of light-weight (DK) multi-coloured thin ribbon wrapped with a multi-coloured mohair yarn (154yd/140m per ball) in pink/yellow mix

needles

1 pair of size 7 (4.5mm) needles

GAUGE

28 sts and 24 rows to 4in (10cm) measured over wave st patt using size 7 (4.5mm) needles

Knit Your Scarf...

Using size 7 (4.5mm) needles and **B**, cast on 39 sts.

Knit 3 rows.

Commence wave stitch patt.

Row 1 RS Using **A**, k to end.

Row 2 Using **A**, p1, (p2tog) twice, *p2, yo, (p1, yo, p1) into next st, yo, p2, p2tog, p3tog, p2tog; rep from * once more, p2, yo, (p1, yo, p1) into next st, yo, p2, (p2tog) twice, p1.

Row 3 Using **A**, k to end, working into back of yos of previous row.

Row 4 Using **A**, as row 2.

Row 5 Using **B**, k to end, working into back of yos of previous row.

Rows 6, 7 and 8 Using **B**, knit to end.

These 8 rows form the wave stitch pattern and are repeated.

Cont in patt until scarf measures 42in (106cm), ending with row 8 of patt.

Using **B**, bind off loosely.

To Finish...

Sew in all ends. Press according to instructions on ball bands.

KNIT NOTE

The wave pattern is worked over a multiple of 12 sts plus 3 extra for the edge stitches; cast on 51 sts for a wider scarf, 75 sts or more for a wrap. Many traditional stitch patterns use increases and decreases to pull the knitted fabric into waves. By adding more stitches between the shaping stitches, a flatter wave would be made; by arranging them close together, like here, a sharper wave is produced. The decreases pull the fabric down into troughs while the increases (yos) form the peaks of the waves.

ROMANTIC ROSES

Everything about this bed throw is gloriously romantic. The colour is a wonderful shade of dark rose in a sumptuous and sensual silk and wool mix that has a delicate sheen and is smooth to the touch. The lacy panels create a glamorous pattern that looks like climbing roses twining up a long stem, and this rose garden design is enhanced by the addition of pretty rose-petal and leaf trimmings. This throw will transform any bedroom into a beautiful boudoir. The pattern for the matching Posy Pillowcase, complete with rambling roses, is given on pages 126–127.

STITCH FOCUS

Experiment by replacing the border with any of the lacy edgings on pages 77–83. Leaf Edging (see page 78) and Lacy Leaf Edging (see page 81) will match the leaf trimmings. Lace Ruffle (see page 83) will create a frilly edge, while Openwork Garter Stitch (see page 77) is a quick way to add a scalloped border.

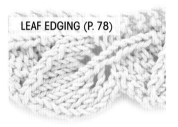

LEAF EDGING (P. 78)

LACY LEAF EDGING (P. 81)

RE-STITCHED

The blank canvas of the stockinette (stocking) stitch background provides a perfect opportunity to show off more delicate stitches.

LACE RUFFLE (P. 83)

OPENWORK GARTER STITCH (P. 77)

ROSE GARDEN THROW

This throw is worked in seven panels; four feature a lace pattern of twisting stems and leaves, and these are separated by plain (stockinette) panels that echo the undulating waves. Each panel is knitted separately and the pieces sewn together at the end. The lace is created by yfwds and decreases (ssk, k2tog, and k3tog; see pages 135–136). Simple roses are added as corsages, and their stems are made from I-cord. The throw is trimmed with a lace border.

MEASUREMENTS
51in (130cm) wide and 63in (160cm) long

GATHER TOGETHER...
Materials
A 19 x 1¾oz (50g) balls of medium-weight (aran) wool/silk yarn (98yd/90m per ball) in dark rose
B 1 x 1¾oz (50g) ball of light-weight (DK) wool yarn (110yd/100m per ball) in dark green
Roses: 1 x 1¾oz (50g) ball of fine-weight (4ply) cotton or wool in each of light pink, dusky pink, dark pink, lilac and light lilac

Needles
1 pair of size 11 (8mm) needles
1 pair of size 3 (3.25mm) needles
2 size 6 (4mm) double-pointed needles

GAUGE
14 sts and 19 rows to 4in (10cm) measured over st st (1 row k, 1 row p) using size 11 (8mm) needles and **A**

Knit Your Throw...
Lace Panel
(Make 4)
Using size 11 (8mm) needles and **A**, cast on 29 sts.
Purl 1 row.
Next Row K13, k2tog, yfwd, k14.
Next Row P.
Rep the last two rows twice more.

Commence lace patt.
Row 1 K3, yfwd, k9, k2tog, yfwd, k2tog, k13.
Row 2 and every foll WS row P to end.
Row 3 K3, yfwd, k1, yfwd, ssk, k6, k2tog, yfwd, k2tog, k13.
Row 5 (K3, yfwd) twice, ssk, k4, k2tog, yfwd, k2tog, k13.
Row 7 K3, yfwd, k5, yfwd, ssk, k2, k2tog, yfwd, k2tog, k13.
Row 9 K3, (yfwd, k1) twice, k3tog tbl, (k1, yfwd) twice, (ssk) twice, yfwd, ssk, k13.
Row 11 (K3, yfwd) twice, k3tog tbl, yfwd, k3, ssk, yfwd, ssk, k13.
Row 13 K3, M1, k1, yfwd, ssk, k1, yfwd, k3tog tbl, yfwd, k2, ssk, yfwd, ssk, k13.
Row 15 K3, M1, k3, yfwd, ssk, k4, ssk, yfwd, ssk, k13.

Row 17 K3, M1, k5, yfwd, ssk, k2, ssk, yfwd, ssk, k13.
Row 19 K3, M1, k7, yfwd, (ssk) twice, yfwd, ssk, k13.
Row 21 K3, M1, k9, yfwd, (ssk) twice, k13.
Row 23 K14, yfwd, ssk, k13.
Row 25 As row 23.
Row 27 As row 23.
Row 29 K13, ssk, yfwd, ssk, k9, yfwd, k3.
Row 31 K13, ssk, yfwd, ssk, k6, k2tog, yfwd, k1, yfwd, k3.
Row 33 K13, ssk, yfwd, ssk, k4, k2tog, (yfwd, k3) twice.
Row 35 K13, ssk, yfwd, ssk, k2, k2tog, yfwd, k5, yfwd, k3.
Row 37 K13, k2tog, yfwd, (k2tog) twice, (yfwd, k1) twice, k3tog, (k1, yfwd) twice, k3.
Row 39 K13, k2tog, yfwd, k2tog, k3, yfwd, k3tog, (yfwd, k3) twice.
Row 41 K13, k2tog, yfwd, k2tog, k2, yfwd, k3tog, yfwd, k1, k2tog, yfwd, k1, M1, k3.
Row 43 K13, k2tog, yfwd, k2tog, k4, k2tog, yfwd, k3, M1, k3.
Row 45 K13, k2tog, yfwd, k2tog, k2, k2tog, yfwd, k5, M1, k3.
Row 47 K13, k2tog, yfwd, (k2tog) twice, yfwd, k7, M1, k3.
Row 49 K13, (k2tog) twice, yfwd, k9, M1, k3.

Row 51 K13, k2tog, yfwd, k14.
Row 53 As row 51.
Row 55 As row 51.
Row 56 P to end.
These 56 rows form the lace patt and
are repeated.
Rep these 56 rows four times more.
Bind off.

Plain Panel
(Make 3)
Using size 11 (8mm) needles and **A**, cast on
21 sts.
Work 6 rows in st st, starting with a k row.
**Row 1 K3, M1, k14, k2tog, k2. 21 sts.
Row 2 P.
Rep rows 1 and 2 ten times more.
Work 6 rows in st st, starting with a k row.
Row 29 K2, ssk, k14, M1, k3. 21 sts.
Row 30 P.
Rep rows 29 and 30 ten times more.
Work 6 rows in st st, starting with a k row.**
Rep from ** to ** four times more.
Bind off.

*The throw is edged with a pretty lace border
that is sewn into place for a final flourish.*

Lace Border
Using size 11 (8mm) needles and **A**, cast on
7 sts.
Row 1 and every foll WS row K2, p to end.
Row 2 K5, yfwd, k2.
Row 4 K3, k2tog, yfwd, k1, yfwd, k2.
Row 6 K2, k2tog, yfwd, k3, yfwd, k2.
Row 8 K1, k2tog, yfwd, k5, yfwd, k2.
Row 10 K1, k2tog, yfwd, k1, k3tog, k1, yfwd,
k2tog, k1.

Row 12 K1, k2tog, yfwd, k3tog, yfwd, k2tog, k1.
Row 14 K1, k2tog, yfwd, k4.
Row 16 As row 14.
The 16 rows form the lace border and are
repeated. Cont in patt until border is of
sufficient length to fit around throw, ending
with row 16 of patt. Bind off.

*The sculptural roses in realistic colours stand
out beautifully against the smooth and lustrous
texture of the knitted throw.*

Small Roses
(Make 15 using rose colours randomly)
Using size 3 (3.25mm) needles, cast on 80 sts.
Work 8 rows in st st, starting with a k row.
Dec Row (K2tog) 40 times. 40 sts.
Dec Row (P2tog) 20 times. 20 sts.
Dec Row (K2tog) 10 times. 10 sts.
Cut yarn leaving a long length. Using a tapestry
needle, thread yarn through sts. Pull up into
gathers. Form the rose by twisting it round and
round from the centre with RS of fabric facing
outwards. Secure with a few sts through all
layers at the base. Leave the long length of yarn
for sewing onto throw.

Large Roses
(Make 5 using rose colours randomly)
Using size 3 (3.25mm) needles, cast on
100 sts.
Work 12 rows in st st, starting with a k row.
Dec Row (K2tog) 50 times. 50 sts.

Dec Row (P2tog) 25 times. 25 sts.
Dec Row (K2tog) 12 times, k1. 13 sts.
Complete as given for Small Roses.

Leaves
(Make 8)
Using size 6 (4mm) needles and **B**, cast on
3 sts.
Row 1 K to end.
Row 2 and every foll WS row K1, p to last
st, k1.
Row 3 (K1, yfwd) twice, k1. 5 sts.
Row 5 K2, yfwd, k1, yfwd, k2. 7 sts.
Row 7 K to end.
Row 9 Ssk, k to last 2 sts, k2tog.
Row 11 As row 9. 3 sts
Row 13 Sk2po.
Cut yarn and thread through rem st.

Stems
Using size 6 (4mm) double-pointed needles
and **B**, cast on 4 sts and work three pieces of
I-cord (see page 117) 24in (60cm) long and
one piece 14in (36cm).

To Finish...
Sew in all ends neatly. Press according to
instructions on ball bands. Sew panels together,
matching wave shapes. Sew border around
edge. Lay the roses on to the throw in three
groups, placing the stems and leaves around
them (refer to the photograph for guidance
– note that one of the three groups of roses
includes two stems). Sew them on to the throw.

POSY PILLOWCASE

The matching pillowcase is made from a single lace panel and simple stockinette. More roses, leaves and the I-cord stem adorn the pillow.

Take care to find shades of yarn for the roses that will really complement the pillowcase. Here I chose realistic colours and used wool yarns for softness and warmth.

MEASUREMENTS
27in (68cm) wide and 20in (51cm) long

GATHER TOGETHER...
Materials
A 6 x 1¾oz (50g) balls of medium-weight (aran) wool/silk yarn (98yd/90m per ball) in dark rose

B 1 x 1¾oz (50g) ball of light-weight (DK) wool yarn (110yd/100m per ball) in dark green

Roses: 1 x 1¾oz (50g) ball of fine-weight (4ply) cotton or wool in each of light pink, dusky pink, dark pink, lilac and light lilac

Needles
1 pair of size 11 (8mm) needles
1 pair of size 3 (3.25mm) needles
2 size 6 (4mm) double-pointed needles

GAUGE
14 sts and 19 rows to 4in (10cm) measured over st st (1 row k, 1 row p) using size 11 (8mm) needles and **A**

Knit Your Pillowcase...
Lace Panel
Using size 11 (8mm) needles and **A**, cast on 29 sts and work as given for Lace Panel of the Rose Garden Throw, repeating 56 rows of patt twice and then rows 1 to 52 once more.
Bind off.

Main Piece
Using size 11 (8mm) needles and **A**, cast on 67 sts.
**Work 6 rows in st st, starting with a k row.
Next Row K to last 4 sts, k2tog, k2.
Next Row P.
Rep the last two rows ten times more. 56 sts.
Work 6 rows in st st, starting with a k row.
Next Row K to last 3 sts, M1, k3.
Next Row P.
Rep the last 2 rows 10 times more.** 67 sts.
Rep from ** to ** twice more.
Work 2 rows in st st.
Bind off.

Border
Using size 11 (8mm) needles and **A**, cast on 7 sts and work as given for the border of the Rose Garden Throw, until border is of sufficient length to fit along edge of lace panel.

Small Roses
Make 5 as given for the Rose Garden Throw, using rose colours randomly.

Large Rose
Make 1 as given for the Rose Garden Throw, choosing a rose colour randomly.

Leaves
Make 2 as given for the Rose Garden Throw.

Stem
Using size 6 (4mm) double-pointed needles and B, cast on 4 sts and work a piece of I-cord (see page 117) 12in (30cm) long.

To Finish...
Sew in all ends neatly. Press according to instructions on ball bands. Sew lace panel on to main piece, matching wave shapes. Sew border along edge of lace panel. Lay the roses on to the pillowcase, placing the stem and leaves around them (refer to the photograph for guidance). Sew them on to the pillowcase. Fold the case in half and join the long seam. Sew the side seam.

IT'S ALL IN THE DETAIL
CASTING ON

Most knitters have their own favoured way of casting on, so I have not specified in the projects which method to use. Cable cast-on makes a very firm, strong edge, making it ideal for bags. However, for many projects you should cast on loosely. If you cast on too tightly, the edge will not stretch sufficiently and may break. Try using a size larger needle to make sure it is loose enough. Remember to change back to the correct size needle to begin knitting.

KNITTING ON

This simple method of casting on needs two needles. Begin by making a slip knot about 6in (15cm) from the end of the yarn and slip it on to a needle held in your left hand. This method produces a loose cast-on edge, ideal for lace fabrics where a hard edge is not necessary.

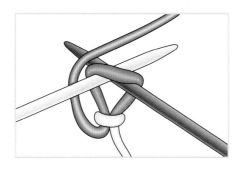

1 Insert the right-hand needle into the slip knot as though to knit it and wrap the yarn around the tip.

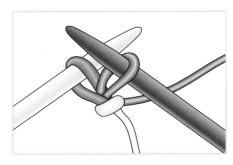

2 Pull a new loop through but do not slip the stitch off the left-hand needle.

3 Place the loop on to the left-hand needle as shown by inserting the left-hand needle into the front of the loop from right to left.

4 Insert the right-hand needle (as though to knit) into the stitch just made and wrap the yarn around the tip. Pull a new loop through and place it on to the left-hand needle.

Repeat step 4 until you have cast on the required number of stitches.

KNITTING ON AND CABLE CAST ON...
These two methods are also used for casting on stitches at the beginning of a row, which usually happens in shaping a garment. To cast on extra stitches in the middle of knitting, work step 4 of the Cable Cast On instructions only, working the first stitch between the next two stitches already on the left-hand needle.

CABLE CAST ON

Work the same as knitting on but instead of going into a stitch the needle goes between stitches. It should be worked quite loosely so the needle slips between stitches easily. This produces a rope-like edge used when working buttonholes where stitches are cast off on one row and cast on again on the next row.

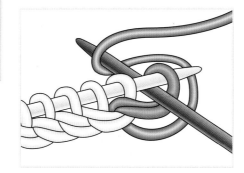

Cast on two stitches using the knitting on method. Insert the right-hand needle between the first and second stitches and wrap the yarn around the tip. When the new loop is pulled through between the stitches, place it on to the left-hand needle as for knitting on, see step 3.

KNIT STITCH

In knitting there are only two stitches to learn: knit (k) and purl (p). All other knitted fabrics are created by combining these two stitches. The knit stitch is the one that all beginners learn first and is very versatile when used on its own. When you knit each row, the fabric you make is garter stitch. It lies flat, is quite a thick fabric and does not curl at the edges, which makes it ideal for bag handles and edgings.

MAKING THE KNIT STITCH – ENGLISH METHOD
Each knit stitch is made up of four easy steps. The yarn is held at the back of the work (the side facing away from you).

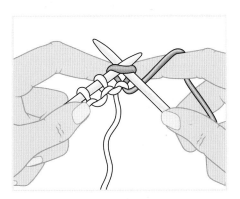

1 Hold the needle with the cast-on stitches in your left hand and insert the right-hand needle into the front of the stitch from left to right.

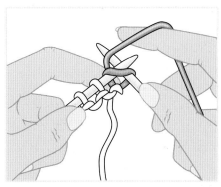

2 Pass the yarn under and around the right-hand needle.

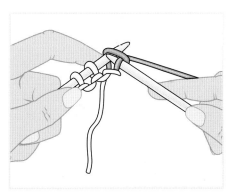

3 Pull the new loop on the right-hand needle through the stitch on the left-hand needle.

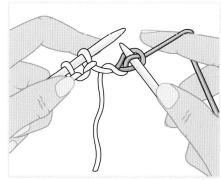

4 Slip the stitch off the left-hand needle. One knit stitch is completed.

Repeat these four steps for each stitch on the left-hand needle. All the stitches on the left-hand needle will be transferred to the right-hand needle, where the new row is formed. At the end of the row, swap the needle with the stitches into your left hand and the empty needle into your right hand to begin the next row.

KNIT STITCH CONTINUED

MAKING THE KNIT STITCH – CONTINENTAL METHOD

In this method the right-hand needle moves to catch the yarn; the yarn is held at the back of the work (the side facing away from you) and is released by the index finger of the left hand. This knit stitch is made up of four steps.

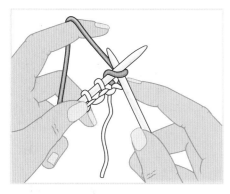

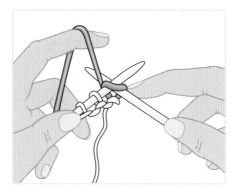

1 Hold the needle with the cast on stitches in your left hand and the yarn over your left index finger. Insert the right-hand needle into the front of the stitch from left to right.

2 Move the right-hand needle down and across the back of the yarn.

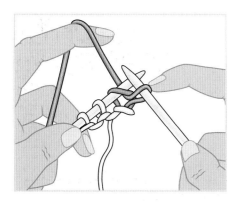

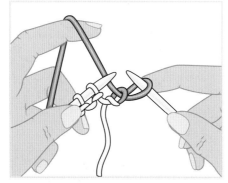

3 Pull the new loop on the right-hand needle through the stitch on the left-hand needle, using the right index finger to hold the new loop if needed.

4 Slip the stitch off the left-hand needle. One knit stitch is completed.

Repeat these four steps for each stitch on the left-hand needle. All the stitches on the left-hand needle will be transferred to the right-hand needle where the new row is formed. At the end of the row, swap the needle with the stitches into your left hand and the empty needle into your right hand, and work the next row in the same way.

PURL STITCH

Purl stitch is just as easy to learn as knit stitch. Once you know both stitches, you can pretty much make anything. One row of knit and one row of purl makes stockinette stitch, which is really helpful for practising your knit and purl; just cast on, work in stockinette stitch and bind off.

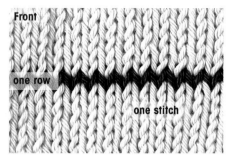

STOCKINETTE STITCH

Stockinette stitch (st st) is formed by knitting one row, purling the next row, and then repeating these two rows.

In the knitting instructions for the projects, stockinette stitch is written as follows:

Row 1 RS Knit.
Row 2 Purl.

Or, the instructions may be:

Work in st st (1 row k, 1 row p), beg with a k row.

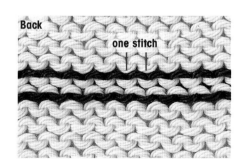

REVERSE STOCKINETTE STITCH

Reverse stockinette stitch (rev st st) is when the back of stockinette stitch fabric is used as the right side. This is commonly used as the background for cables, but can also be used as the right side of fabrics knitted in fancy yarns, such as faux fur or fashion yarns. This is because most of the textured effect of the yarn remains on the reverse side of the fabric.

MAKING THE PURL STITCH – ENGLISH METHOD

Each purl stitch is made up of four easy steps. The yarn is held at the front of the work (the side facing you).

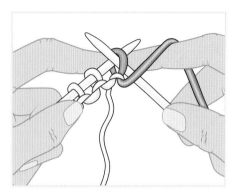

1 Hold the needle with the cast-on stitches in your left hand, and insert the right-hand needle into the front of the stitch from right to left.

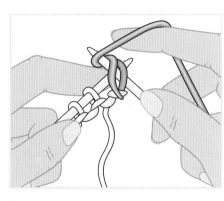

2 Pass the yarn over and around the right-hand needle.

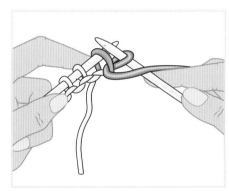

3 Pull the new loop on the right-hand needle through the stitch on the left-hand needle.

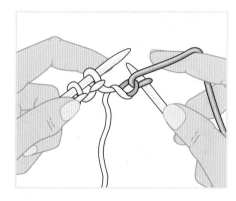

4 Slip the stitch off the left-hand needle. One stitch is completed.

Repeat these four steps for each stitch on the left-hand needle. All the stitches on the left-hand needle will be transferred to the right-hand needle, where the new purl row is formed. At the end of the row, swap the needle with the stitches into your left hand and the empty needle into your right hand to begin the next row.

131

PURL STITCH CONTINUED

MAKING THE PURL STITCH – CONTINENTAL METHOD

In purl stitch the yarn is held at the front of the work (the side facing you) and is made up of four steps.

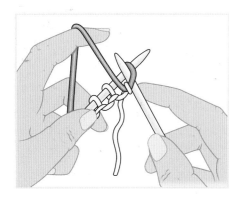

1 Hold the needle with the cast on stitches in your left hand, and insert the right-hand needle into the front of the stitch from right to left, keeping the yarn at the front of the work.

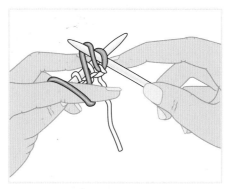

2 Move the right-hand needle from right to left behind the yarn and then from left to right in front of the yarn. Pull your left index finger down in front of the work to keep the yarn taut.

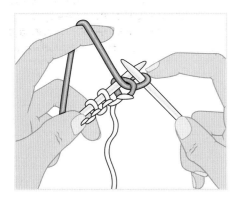

3 Pull the new loop on the right-hand needle through the stitch on the left-hand needle, using the right index finger to hold the new loop if needed.

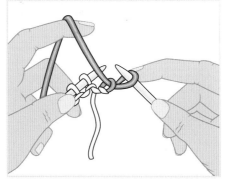

4 Slip the stitch off the left-hand needle. Return the left index finger to its position above the needle. One stitch is completed.

Repeat these four steps for each stitch on the left-hand needle. All the stitches on the left-hand needle will be transferred to the right-hand needle where the new purl row is formed. At the end of the row, swap the needle with the stitches into your left hand and the empty needle into your right hand, and work the next row in the same way.

BINDING OFF

Unless specifically instructed to do otherwise, you should bind off in pattern – for example, knitwise on the right side of a piece knitted in stockinette stitch. The various methods are explained right and below. The bound-off edge should not be too tight, otherwise it will pull the knitted fabric in. This is important when binding off an edge that will show, such as the top of a bag or edge of a pocket. If you tend to bind off tightly, try using a needle a size larger than that used for the knitted fabric.

KNIT PERFECT

When you wish to stop knitting, but aren't ready to bind off yet, always finish the complete row. Finishing in the middle of a row will stretch the stitches and they may slide off the needle. If you need to put your knitting aside for several weeks or even months and do not have time to finish the piece beforehand, mark on the pattern or make a note of where you have got to. If you are working in a regular pattern such as stockinette stitch, when restarting again it is worth unravelling a couple of rows and reknitting them, as stitches left over time on the needles can become stretched and leave an unsightly ridge where you stopped.

BIND OFF KNITWISE

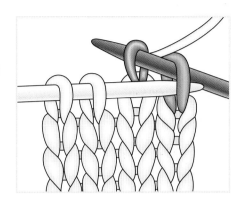

1 Knit two stitches, and insert the tip of the left-hand needle into the front of the first stitch on the right-hand needle.

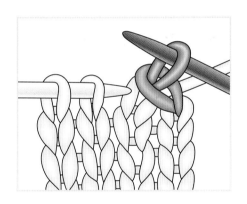

3 One stitch is left on the right-hand needle.

BIND OFF PURLWISE
To bind off on a purl row, simply purl the stitches instead of knitting them.

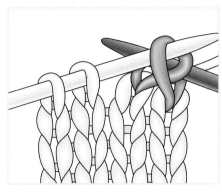

2 Lift this stitch over the second stitch and off the needle.

4 Knit the next stitch and lift the second stitch over this and off the needle. Continue in this way until one stitch remains on the right-hand needle. Cut the yarn (leaving a length long enough to sew in), thread the end through the last stitch and slip it off the needle. Pull the yarn end to tighten the stitch.

BIND OFF IN PATTERN
To bind off in a pattern such as rib, you must knit the knit stitches and purl the purl stitches of the rib. If you are working a pattern of cable stitches, you bind off in pattern; again, knit the knit stitches and purl the purl stitches.

INCREASING STITCHES

Some of the projects in this book call for some shaping – otherwise all the items you ever knit would be square or rectangular. There are several ways to increase stitches. In some instructions I have specified which increase to use, in others I haven't. Try to keep your increase edge as neat as possible if it will be seen on the finished item. It always looks neater if the increase stitch is worked one stitch in from the edge.

MAKE 1 (M1)

This increase is used when increasing stitches after a rib, such as in the Beret (see page 109). It is also used for shaping the thumb gusset on the matching Gloves (see pages 110–111). Use both the right- and left-twisting versions for a neat finish. The new stitch is made between two existing stitches using the horizontal thread that lies between them.

To twist M1 to the left

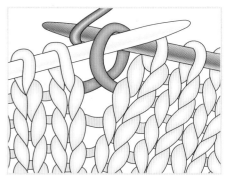   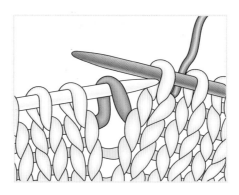

1 Knit to the point where the increase is to be made. Insert the tip of the left-hand needle under the running thread from front to back.

2 Knit this loop through the back to twist it. By twisting it you prevent a hole appearing where the made stitch is.

To twist M1 to the right

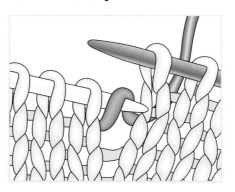   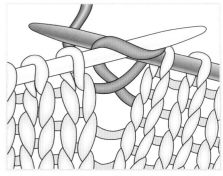

1 Knit to the point where the increase is to be made. Insert the tip of the left-hand needle under the running thread from back to front.

2 Knit this loop through the front to twist it.

INCREASING STITCHES CONTINUED

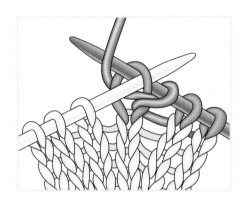

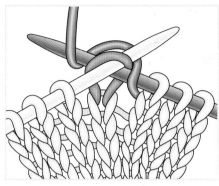

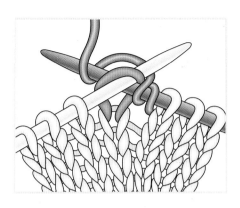

KNIT INTO FRONT AND BACK (KF&B)
Knit into the front of the stitch as usual. Do not slip the stitch off the left-hand needle, but knit into it again through the back of the loop. Then slip the original stitch off the left-hand needle.

PURL INTO FRONT AND BACK (PF&B)
Work as given for kf&b, but purl into the front and back instead.

YO (YFWD) BETWEEN TWO STITCHES
This produces a hole so is used for small buttonholes, or as a decorative increase such as on leaves. Bring the yarn forward between the two needles. Knit the next stitch, taking the yarn over the right-hand needle.

MULTIPLE YARN OVERS
These are used to make the bigger holes in the Lacy Lovely bag (pages 116–118).

YO TWICE
Wrap the yarn around the needle twice. On the return row, knit then purl into the 2 yo.

YO 3 TIMES
Wrap the yarn around the needle three times. On the return row, work as given in the pattern instructions.

DECREASING STITCHES

Decreases are used in many of the projects, either to shape them or in one of their details. They are also used in stitch patterns and to form buttonholes.

DECREASING ONE STITCH

There are a number of ways to decrease one stitch.

K2tog

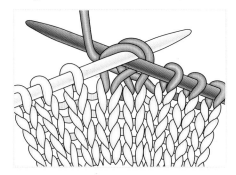

Knit to where the decrease is to be, insert the right-hand needle (as though to knit) through the next two stitches and knit them together as one stitch.

P2tog

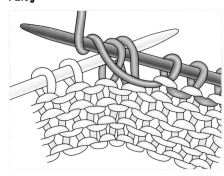

Purl to where the decrease is to be, insert the right-hand needle (as though to purl) through the next two stitches and purl them together as one stitch.

ssk or k2tog tbl

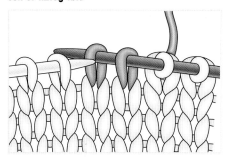

1 Slip two stitches knitwise one at a time from left-hand needle to right-hand needle (they will be twisted).

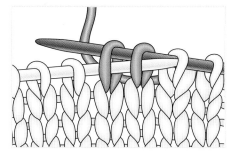

2 Insert the left-hand needle from left to right through the fronts of these two stitches and knit together as one stitch.

DECREASING TWO STITCHES AT ONCE

There are various ways of decreasing two stitches at once.

K3tog

Work as k2tog, but knit three stitches together instead of two.

P3tog

Work as p2tog, but purl three stitches together instead of two.

K3tog tbl

Work as ssk (or k2tog tbl), but slip three stitches instead of two and knit them together.

P3tog tbl

Work as ssp, but slip three stitches instead of two and purl them together through the backs of the loops.

SK2PO

This stands for: slip one, knit two together, pass slipped stitch over. Slip the next stitch onto the right-hand needle, knit the next two stitches together, and lift the slipped stitch over the k2tog and off the needle.

ssp

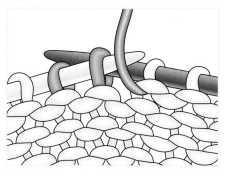

1 Slip two stitches knitwise, one at a time, from the left-hand needle to the right-hand needle (they will be twisted), pass these two stitches back to the left-hand needle in this twisted way.

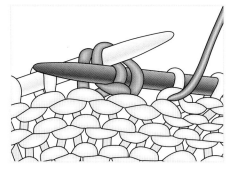

2 Purl these two stitches together through the back loops.

LACE KNITTING

The holes in lace knitting are made by working a yarn over. This makes (increases) a stitch so it has to be accompanied by a decrease. The way you work a yarn over depends on the stitches either side of it. In patterns, where yarn over (yo) is given, you decide which yarn over method to use. Some patterns will tell you which one to use.

KNIT PERFECT

When working a lace pattern you may find it helpful to place a marker (make several slip knot loops of a contrasting colour yarn) between each repeat, where the asterisks are, and slip them on every row. Then you can keep track of each small repeat instead of having to work back through a long row of stitches if you make a mistake.

WORKING A YARN OVER

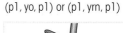

Between two knit stitches
(k1, yo, k1) or (k1, yfwd, k1)

Bring the yarn forward (yfwd or yf) between the two needles. Knit the next stitch, taking the yarn over the right-hand needle.

Between two purl stitches
(p1, yo, p1) or (p1, yrn, p1)

Take the yarn back over the right-hand needle and forward between the needles to bring yarn round needle (yrn). Purl the next stitch.

Between knit and purl stitches
(k1, yo, p1) or (k1, yfrn, p1)

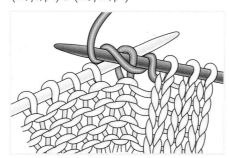

Bring the yarn forward between the two needles, take it back over the right-hand needle and forward again between the two needles – yarn forward and round needle (yfrn). Purl the next stitch.

Between purl and knit stitches
(p1, yo, k1) or (p1, yon, k1)

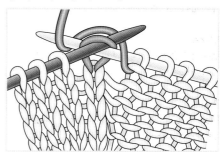

Take the yarn back over the right-hand needle – yarn over needle (yon). Knit the next stitch.

CABLES

Cables are simply a way of twisting two sets of stitches or carrying stitches across the fabric. There are two ways of moving the stitches; cabling and crossing. Stitches are cabled when all the stitches are knitted, but stitches are crossed when knit stitches are moved over a background of purl stitches. In patterns, cables are twisted to the back or front, while crossed stitches move right or left.

The two techniques to learn are moving the stitches at the back and moving them at the front. This is done by holding the stitches on a cable needle either at the back or the front of the work. This simple cable twists two sets of knit stitches, using four stitches.

CABLE FOUR FRONT (C4F)

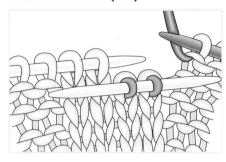

1 Slip the next two stitches from the left-hand needle on to a cable needle and hold at the front of the work.

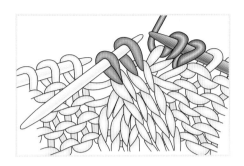

2 Knit the next two stitches on the left-hand needle, then knit the two stitches from the cable needle.

CABLE FOUR BACK (C4B)

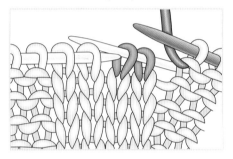

1 Slip the next two stitches from the left-hand needle on to a cable needle and hold at the back of the work.

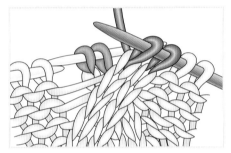

2 Knit the next two stitches on the left-hand needle, then knit the two stitches from the cable needle.

BASIC ABBREVIATIONS FOR CABLES...

C4F	cable four front
C4B	cable four back
Cr4L	cross four left
Cr4R	cross four right

When following a pattern with cables, the designer will explain how to work the cables under special abbreviations at the start of the pattern.

MORE CABLES...

C6F or C6B is worked by slipping three stitches on to the cable needle and then knitting three stitches. C8F or C8B is worked with four stitches in each part of the cable. The more stitches there are in a cable, the more rows there are between twists. So C4F or C4B has three rows straight, C6F or C6B has five rows straight and so on. To make a looser cable, work more rows straight between twists.

TWISTED STITCHES

Single stitches can be twisted over each other without using a cable needle. As in cables, two knit stitches can be cabled to the right or the left. Twisted stitches can also be crossed (one knit stitch moving over a purl stitch) to the right or left.

Twisted cables – right twist (RT)

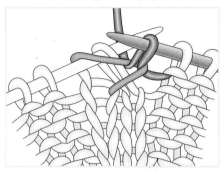

1 Insert the right-hand needle into the second stitch on the left-hand needle and knit it. Don't slip this stitch off the needle.

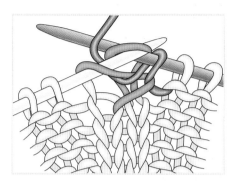

2 Knit the first stitch on the left-hand needle and slip both stitches on to the right-hand needle.

Twisted cables – left twist (LT)

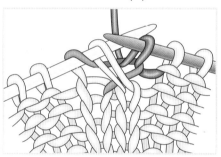

1 Insert the right-hand needle into front of the second stitch on the left-hand needle, working behind the first stitch, and knit it. Don't slip this stitch off the needle.

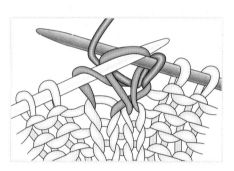

2 Knit the first stitch on the left-hand needle and slip both stitches on to the right-hand needle.

BASIC ABBREVIATIONS FOR TWISTED STITCHES...

RT	twisted cables – right twist
LT	twisted cables – left twist
Cr2R	crossed stitches – cross right
Cr2L	crossed stitches – cross left

When following a pattern with twisted stitches, the designer will explain how to work the stitches under special abbreviations at the start of the pattern.

READING KNITTING PATTERNS

A knitting pattern tells you how to knit and make up a knitted project. The instructions use shorthand phrases and abbreviations, otherwise they would be far too long. The abbreviations used in this book appear in a list on page 141 with an explanation of what they mean. Many are commonly used, such as k and p. Others refer to special stitches, like C4F. These are explained in this technique section or in the pattern itself.

KNIT PERFECT

Throughout this book, any special instructions that are required to complete a project are provided separately from the main project instructions.

SPECIAL INSTRUCTIONS

In some patterns, instructions for the cable panels are put outside the main project instructions. This is because these panels would make the project instructions very long and complicated, and a lot of information would be repeated. The panel is set within a group of stitches; keep following the pattern panel while working your way through the project instructions. For example: **Row 1** (K1, p1) twice, C4F, p2, work row 1 of panel A, p2, C4B, p2, work row 1 of panel B, p2, C4F, p2, work row 1 of panel C, p2, C4B, (p1, k1) twice.

WORKING FROM CHARTS

Most of the stitch patterns in the Stitch Library section give both written and charted instructions. In the chart one square represents one stitch and a line of stitches represents one row. The rows are numbered: right-side rows are odd numbers and are read from right to left; wrong-side rows are even numbers and are read from left to right. Start knitting from the bottom right-hand corner of the chart at row 1.

Fair Isle or intarsia patterns are also usually worked from a chart. In this case there are usually very few written instructions, apart from how many stitches to cast on and any actions that are not included in the chart. Sometimes the chart will show any shaping that has to be done. Fair Isle and intarsia charts are worked in the same way as other charts, starting at the bottom right-hand corner at row 1.

COMMON SHORTHAND PHRASES

You will see some common shorthand phrases appearing in the pattern instructions. These include the following:

Cont as set Instead of repeating the same instructions over and over, the pattern tells you to continue working as previously told. For example:

Cont in cable patt as set, commencing with row 5 of panels, until flap measures approx 11in (28cm) from beg.

Keeping patt correct Continue with a stitch pattern, keeping it correctly worked over the correct number of stitches, while doing something that may interfere with the stitch pattern. For example: Keeping texture patt correct, dec 1 st (as set on row 40) at each end of every foll 6th row to 55 sts.

Work as given for This is used to avoid repeating instructions; it can be used within one set of instructions or to show how to work another version of the same item. For example: Work as given for the Lacy Lovely bag (see pages 116–118), omitting the drawstring strap.

* repeat directions following * as many times as indicated or until end of row. For example: **Row 1** K1, *p1, k1; rep from * to end.

** usually appears at the beginning or at the beginning and the end of a section of instructions and indicates that several rows of instructions should be repeated. For example: Work as given for first strap from ** to **.

( ) you should repeat instructions in round brackets the number of times indicated. For example: K1, (ssk, k5) 7 times, ssk, k6.

IMPERIAL AND METRIC MEASUREMENTS

Note that the patterns are written in both imperial (inches and ounces) and metric (centimetres and grams) measurements. You should stick to one or the other; some imperial to metric measurements are not exact conversions.

ABBREVIATIONS

alt	alternate
approx	approximately
beg	begin/beginning
cm	centimetre(s)
cont	continue
dec(s)	decrease(s)/decreasing
DK	double knitting
foll	following
g	gram
g st	garter stitch (knit every row)
in(s)	inch(es)
inc(s)	increase(s)/increasing
k	knit
kf&b	knit into the front and back of a stitch (1 stitch increased)
k2tog	knit 2 stitches together (1 stitch decreased)
k3tog	knit 3 stitches together (1 stitch decreased)
LH	left hand
LT	left twist
m	metre(s)
mm	millimetre(s)
M1	make one by picking up the strand lying between the sts and knit into the back of it (increase 1 stitch)
MB	make a bobble
oz	ounces
p	purl
patt(s)	pattern(s)
pf&b	purl into the front and back of a stitch (1 stitch increased)
psso	pass slipped stitch over
p2tog	purl 2 stitches together (1 stitch decreased)
p3tog	purl 3 stitches together (2 stitches decreased)
rem	remain/ing
rep(s)	repeat(s)
rev st st	reverse stocking stitch (1 row purl, 1 row knit) (US: reverse stockinette stitch)
RH	right hand
RS	right side
RT	right twist

skpo	slip 1 stitch, knit 1 stitch, pass slipped stitch over (1 stitch decreased)
sk2po	slip 1 stitch, knit 2 stitches, pass slipped stitch over (2 stitches decreased)
sl	slip
sl st	slip stitch
sl 1	slip 1 stitch
sl 1k	slip 1 stitch knitwise
sl 1p	slip 1 stitch purlwise
sl2tog-k1-psso	slip 2 stitches together, knit 1 stitch, pass 2 slipped stitches over (2 stitches decreased)
ssk	slip 2 stitches one at a time, knit 2 slipped stitches together (1 stitch decreased)
ssp	slip 2 stitches one at a time, purl 2 slipped stitches together through the back of the loop (1 stitch decreased)
st(s)	stitch(es)
st st	stocking stitch (1 row knit, 1 row purl) (US: stockinette stitch)
tbl	through back of loop
tog	together
WS	wrong side
wyib	with yarn in back
wyif	with yarn in front
yd(s)	yard(s)
yfrn	yarn forward and round needle
yfwd	yarn forward
yo	yarn over
yrn	yarn round needle
*	repeat directions following * as many times as indicated or until the end of the row
[ ]	instructions in square brackets refer to larger sizes
( )	repeat instructions in round brackets the number of times indicated

In the instructions for the projects, I have favoured US knitting terms. Refer to this box for the UK equivalent.

US TERM	UK TERM
bind off	cast off
gauge	tension
stockinette stitch	stocking stitch
reverse stockinette stitch	reverse stocking stitch
seed stitch	moss stitch
moss stitch	double moss stitch

YARNS USED

Below are listed the specific yarns that were used for the projects in this book, should you wish to recreate them exactly as we have. Yarn companies frequently discontinue colours or yarns and replace them with new yarns. Therefore, you may find that some of the yarns or colours below are no longer available. However, by referring to the yarn descriptions on the project pages, you should have no trouble finding a substitute.

SUBSTITUTING YARNS

To work out how much replacement yarn you need, just follow these simple steps. Use them for each colour of yarn used in the project.
1 The number of balls of the recommended yarn x the number of yards/metres per ball = A
2 The number of yards/metres per ball of the replacement yarn = B
3 A ÷ B = number of balls of replacement yarn.

PAGE 98 PATCHWORK CUSHION

1 × 1¾oz/50g ball of Rowan Handknit Cotton DK (100% cotton – 93yd/85m per ball) in colour **A** 204 Chime
1 × 1¾oz/50g ball of Rowan Wool Cotton DK (50% merino wool/50% cotton – 123yd/113m per ball) in colours:
B 933 Violet, **C** 952 Hiss, **D** 951 Tender
2 × 1¾oz/50g balls of Debbie Bliss Cotton DK (100% cotton – 92yd/84m per ball) in colour **E** 13020 Bright Green

PAGE 100 PLACE MAT AND COASTER

3 × 1¾oz/50g balls of Debbie Bliss Cotton DK (100% cotton – 92yd/84m per ball) in colour 13020 Bright Green

PAGE 101 CABLE THROW

3 × 3½oz/100g hanks of Rowan Rowanspun Chunky (100% pure new wool – 142yd/130m per hank) in colours:
A 981 Pebble, **B** 982 Green Water, **C** 983 Cardamom, 2 × 3½oz/100g hanks in colour **D** 984 Silver

PAGE 102 CROSSOVER CABLES

11 × 3½oz (100g) hanks of Colinette Skye (100% wool – 151yd/138m per hank) in colour 75 moss

PAGE 106 CASHMERE CHIC SET
Whole Set
7 x 1¾oz (50g) balls of Rowan Classic Yarns Cashsoft DK (57% wool/33% microfibre/10% cashmere – 142yd/130m per ball) in colour 521
Scarf
3 x 1¾oz (50g) balls of above yarn
Beret
2 x 1¾oz (50g) balls of above yarn
Corsage
1 x 1¾oz (50g) balls of above yarn
Gloves
2 x 1¾oz (50g) balls of above yarn

PAGE 112 FALLING LEAVES

A 2 x 1¾oz (50g) balls of Rowan Scottish Tweed DK (100% wool – 123yd/113m per ball) in colour 15
B 6 x 8m skeins of DMC Tapestry Wool (100% wool) in colours 7922, 7947, 7740, 7125, 7946, 7214

PAGE 116 LACY LOVELY

1 x 3½oz (100g) ball of Sirdar Pure Cotton 4ply (100% cotton – 370yd/338m per ball) in colour 21

PAGE 119 MAKING WAVES

A 1 x 1¾oz (50g) balls of Jaeger Matchmaker DK (100% wool – 131yd/120m per ball) in colour 899
B 1 x 1¾oz (50g) balls of Louisa Harding Impression (84% nylon/16% mohair – 154yd/140m per ball) in colour 02

PAGE 122 ROMANTIC ROSES
Rose Garden Throw
A 19 x 1¾oz (50g) balls of Lang Silkdream (50% merino/50% silk – 98yd/90m per ball) in shade 66
B 1 x 1¾oz (50g) ball of Rare Yarns Essentials Cocoon Jade (70% merino/15% alpaca/7.5% silk/7.5% mohair – 110yd/100m per ball) in Jade

Roses: 1 x 1¾oz (50g) ball of each of:
Sirdar Luxury Soft Cotton 4ply (100% cotton – 225yd/208m per ball) in shade 661
Rowan 4ply Cotton (100% cotton – 186yd/170m per ball) in shade 120
Patons Diploma Gold 4ply (55% wool/25% acrylic/20% nylon – 201yd/184m per ball) in each of shades 4294 and 4249
Patons Cotton 4ply (100% cotton – 361yd/330m per ball) in shade 1701

Posy Pillowcase
A 6 x 1¾oz (50g) balls of Lang Silkdream (50% merino/50% silk – 98yd/90m per ball) in shade 66
All other yarns same as Rose Garden Throw

SUPPLIERS

Contact the manufacturers for your local stockist or go to their websites for stockist and mail order information.

Colinette
www.colinette.co.uk
(USA) Unique Kolours
28 North Bacton Hill Road,
Malvern, PA 19355
Tel: (800) 252 3934
www.uniquekolours.com
email: uniquekolo@aol.com
(UK) Colinette Yarns Ltd
Banwy Workshops,
Llanfair Caereinion, SY21 0SG
Tel: 01938 810128
e-mail: feedback@colinette.com

Debbie Bliss
www.debbieblissonline.com
(USA) Knitting Fever Inc.
315 Bayview Avenue,
Amityville, NY 11701
Tel: 001 516 5463600
e-mail:
admin@knittingfever.com
www.knittingfever.com
(UK) Designer Yarns Ltd
Units 8–10 Newbridge Industrial
Estate, Pitt Street, Keighley,
West Yorkshire, BD21 4PQ
Tel: 01535 664222
www.designeryarns.uk.com
(AUS) Prestige Yarns Pty Ltd
PO Box 39, Bulli, NSW 2516
Tel: 02 4285 6669
e-mail: info@prestigeyarns.com
www.prestigeyarns.com

DMC
(USA) The DMC Corporation
77 South Hackensack Avenue, Bldg
10F, South Kearney, NJ 07032-4688
Tel: 973 589 0606
www.dmc-usa.com
(UK) DMC Creative World Ltd
Pullman Road, Wigston,
Leicester, LE18 2DY
Tel: 0116 281 1040
www.dmc.com
(AUS) For a list of stockists go to
their website at www.dmc.com

GGH
www.ggh-garn.de
(USA) My Muench Yarns Inc
1323 Scott Street,
Petaluma, CA 94954-1135
Tel: (707) 763 9377
e-mail: info@muenchyarns.com
www.muenchyarns.com
(UK) Loop
41 Cross Street,
London, N1 2BB
Tel: 020 7288 1160
e-mail: info@loop.gb.com
www.loopknittingshop.com

Louisa Harding
www.louisaharding.co.uk
(USA) Knitting Fever Inc.
315 Bayview Avenue,
Amityville, NY 11701
Tel: 001 516 5463600
e-mail: admin@knittingfever.com
www.knittingfever.com
(UK) Designer Yarns Ltd
Units 8–10 Newbridge Industrial
Estate, Pitt Street, Keighley,
West Yorkshire, BD21 4PQ
Tel: 01535 664222
email: enquiries@designeryarns.uk.com
www.designeryarns.uk.com

Noro
www. esiakunoro.com
(USA) Knitting Fever Inc.
315 Bayview Avenue,
Amityville, NY 11701
Tel: 001 516 5463600
e-mail: admin@knittingfever.com
www.knittingfever.com
(UK) Designer Yarns Ltd,
Units 8–10 Newbridge Industrial
Estate, Pitt Street, Keighley,
West Yorkshire, BD21 4PQ
Tel: 01535 664222
www.designeryarns.uk.com
(AUS) Prestige Yarns Pty Ltd
PO Box 39, Bulli, NSW 2516
Tel: +61 02 4285 6669
e-mail: info@prestigeyarns.com
www.prestigeyarns.com

Patons
320 Livingstone Avenue South,
Listowel, Ontario, Canada, N4W 3H3
Tel: 1-888-368-8401
www.patonsyarns.com
(UK) Coats Crafts UK
PO Box 22, Lingfield House,
McMullen Road, Darlington,
County Durham, DL1 1YQ
Tel: 01325 394237
e-mail: consumer.ccuk@coats.com
www.coatscrafts.co.uk

The Rare Yarns Company
The Grape Escape Complex,
McShanes Road, RD1 Richmond
Nelson, New Zealand
Tel: 3 544 0063
e-mail: info@rareyarns.com.au
www.rareyarns.com.au

Rowan
www.knitrowan.com
(USA) Westminster Fibers Inc
165 Ledge Street, Nashua, New
Hampshire 03060
Tel: (603) 886 5041/5043
www.westminsterfibers.com
e-mail: info@westminsterfibers.com
(UK) Rowan
Green Lane Mill, Holmfirth, HD9 2DX
Tel: 01484 681881
e-mail: mail@knitrowan.com
**(AUS) Australian Country Spinners
Pty Ltd**
Level 7, 409 St. Kilda Road,
Melbourne, Victoria 3004
Tel: (03) 9380 3888
email: tkohut@auspinners.com.au

Rowan Classic Yarns (RCY)
www.ryclassic.com
(USA) Westminster Fibers Inc
165 Ledge Street, Nashua, New
Hampshire 03060
Tel: (603) 886 5041/5043
www.westminsterfibers.com
e-mail: info@westminsterfibers.com
(UK) RYC
Green Lane Mill, Holmfirth, HD9 2BR
Tel: 01484 681881
e-mail: mail@ryclassic.com
**(AUS) Australian Country Spinners
Pty Ltd**
Level 7, 409 St. Kilda Road,
Melbourne, Victoria 3004
Tel: (03) 9380 3888
email: tkohut@auspinners.com.au

Sirdar
www.sirdar.co.uk
(USA) Knitting Fever Inc
315 Bayview Avenue, Amityville,
NY 11701
Tel: 001 516 5463600
e-mail: admin@knittingfever.com
www.knittingfever.com
(UK) Sirdar Spinning Ltd
Flanshaw Lane, Alverthorpe,
Wakefield, WF2 9ND
Tel: 01924 371501
e-mail: enquiries@sirdar.co.uk
(AUS) Creative Images
PO Box 106, Hastings, Victoria 3915
Tel: 03 5979 1555
e-mail: creative@peninsula.starway.
net.au

Twilleys
www.twilleys.co.uk
(UK) Twilleys of Stamford
Roman Mill, Stamford, PE9 1BG
Tel: 01780 752661
e-mail: twilleys@tbramsden.co.uk

INDEX